LETTERS FROM DUBLIN, EASTER 1916

Alfred Fannin's Diary of the 1916 Rising

Letters from Dublin, Easter 1916:
Alfred Fannin's Diary
of the Rising

Edited by
Adrian and Sally Warwick-Haller

IRISH ACADEMIC PRESS

Published by
IRISH ACADEMIC PRESS
Kill Lane, Blackrock, Co. Dublin, Ireland
and in North America
IRISH ACADEMIC PRESS
c/o ISBS, 5804 NE Hassalo Street, Portland, OR 97213.

A catalogue record for this title
is available from the British Library.

ISBN 0–7165–2559–3

Printed in Ireland
by ßetaprint Ltd, Dublin.

To the memory of Eustace Fannin (1907–85)
and S.W. Warwick–Haller (1908–94),
lifelong friends

ACKNOWLEDGMENTS

We would like to thank the following for the help they have given us: the Trustees and staff of the National Library of Ireland, the Manuscript Room of Trinity College Dublin, the *Irish Times*, Michael Adams and the staff of the Irish Academic Press, Lionel Booth, Stine Brennan, Joseph Clarke, Annette Fowler, Penny Gibbon, Sheila Harbison, Professor J.B. Lyons, T.P. O'Neill and Dr Christopher Woods. We wish to express our gratitude to Kingston University for the financial help they gave towards the cost of research in Dublin. We would also like to thank Brynhild McConnell and her sons, Allan and David, for giving us permission to publish the Fannin 'diary' and for supplying us with photographs.

Above all, our greatest thanks go to Brynhild for her keen interest, encouragement and being a constant source of knowledge.

CONTENTS

LIST OF ILLUSTRATIONS   viii

INTRODUCTION   1

TEXT OF THE DIARY, WITH NOTES

Letter of 25 April – 6 May 1916   13

Letter of 10 May 1916   47

SELECT BIBLIOGRAPHY   53

LIST OF ILLUSTRATIONS

Dublin after 1916 Rising, O'Connell Street   *cover*

32 Herbert Park   5

Fannin's of Grafton Street   5

Map of Dublin in 1916   12

Fannin Family Tree   15

The Fannin Family at 32, Herbert Park   18

Alfred Fannin   29

Edward and Nora Fannin   30

Dublin after the 1916 Rising,
North Earl Street; Sackville Street and Eden Quay   39

First page of Alfred Fannin's 'diary'   50

INTRODUCTION

On Tuesday 25 April 1916, Alfred Fannin, managing director of the family surgical and medical supply business in Grafton Street (in the centre of Dublin) sat down to write to his brother, Edward, who was stationed with the Royal Army Medical Corps in Malta for almost all the First World War. As he told 'Ed', he had time on his hands and was remaining at home, in Herbert Park, South Dublin, because events in the city made it impossible for him to get into work as normal. Thus began a day-by-day account of the Dublin Easter Rising. This was duly posted to Edward Fannin on 6 May along with copies of the daily papers, and was followed up by a letter four days later. In his covering note of 6 May Alfred asked his brother to keep the letter for him – a request which was fortunately carried out. The 'diary' of the Rising was carefully preserved to be passed on to Alfred's son, Dr Eustace Fannin, who in the mid-1980s, shortly before his death in 1985, showed it to the present editors and expressed the hope that some day the record could be published. His cousin, Brynhild McConnell (Edward's daughter) and her two sons have kindly agreed that this should be done.

Alfred Fannin immediately recognized that what was occurring was of considerable significance: 'There has been nothing in Dublin like this in our generation', he wrote at the end of his first main paragraph.[1] Other Dubliners showed a similar response: that something momentous was afoot and this should be recorded for posterity. One account by Mrs Arthur Mitchell, a neighbour of the Fannins, opens with the words: 'My dear Flora, I feel I must begin to tell you current events which will probably be history in a very short time.'[2] The most famous narrative of all was written by the poet and novelist James Stephens, which was based on his own observations recorded at the time, and which has seen several editions in print. The area where Stephens witnessed the Rising, largely in the vicinity of St Stephen's Green, overlaps with the part of Dublin to which Alfred Fannin restricted himself, with his shop at the top of Grafton Street. The manuscript collections of Trinity College Dublin and the National Library of Ireland have a number of accounts, though some are written after the event, or a few days into the Rising. Several, like Fannin's, take the form of a letter to a close relative; John Dillon's diary, for instance, was addressed to his mother-in-law, Lady Mathew. But Dillon's is not really a first-hand record as he was confined to his home in North Dublin for the week, and thus had to rely on the testimony of others who had travelled round the city. One narrative in particular could be compared to Alfred Fannin's: that written to her sister Flora by Mrs Arthur Mitchell, who like the Fannins lived in Herbert Park. It is also interesting to contrast the two responses from a gender perspective, and one is reminded of James Stephens' comment that:

> Men met and talked volubly, but they said nothing that indicated a personal desire or belief. They asked for and exchanged the latest news, or, rather, rumour, and while expressions were frequent of astonishment at the suddenness and completeness of the occurrence, no expression of opinion for or against was anywhere formulated . . . The women were less guarded, or, perhaps, knew they had less to fear. Most of the female opinion I heard was not alone unfavourable but actively and viciously hostile to the rising. This was noticeable among the best dressed of our population . . .

While Alfred Fannin wrote in a more detached, down-to-earth tone, Mrs Mitchell was explicit in her expression of horror at the turn of events, and wrote of 'the terrible tales heard all day' and the 'awfulness' of the experience.[3]

Though both Mrs Mitchell and Alfred Fannin appreciated the gravity of the situation, neither of them had any glimmer of the consequences that would flow from the Rising. '1916' has traditionally been seen as probably the most significant occurrence in modern Irish history, setting in motion events and changes in attitudes in Ireland that led directly to independence from Britain. However, a role must also be attributed to the impact of the First World War and to the example set by Carson and the Ulster Volunteers' resistance to the prospect of Home Rule. Both these developments helped to make the espousal of violence and 'blood sacrifice' more acceptable; it was part of the rhetoric of the times. Certainly, the Rising bore all the hallmarks of a sacrificial gesture, since the strategy for Dublin had serious military weaknesses.[4] However, the more commonly held view that the Rising was actually *planned* as a blood

sacrifice rather than as a *coup d'état* has been questioned; J.J.
suggested that Pearse had conceived of the Rising as a significant, ⅃
event, with the vision of a military victory as the goal. What occu.   ⌐ ᴜⁱⁱ
Easter Monday was not the Rising that had been planned, and the
hopelessness of the situation (the overwhelming odds, the confusion
surrounding the beginning of the Rising, and the fact that it was very
largely confined to Dublin) transformed it into a blood sacrifice.[5]
Historians in the last few decades have also stressed the need to shift the
hitherto almost exclusive focus on the leaders of the Rising towards, for
instance, the position of the Irish Parliamentary Party, the attitude of
the Church, the role of women, and to the impact on the lives of ordinary
people.

The response of Dubliners to the Rising has been a key issue in the
intepretation of its impact. Most historians agree that the initial attitude
appeared to be one of hostility, of betrayal of the Irishmen who were
fighting in Europe; the rumours that circulated in the press and among
the public at large during Easter Week about German involvement would
have added considerably to the opposition to the Rising. Thus it is argued
that it was the British reply to the Rising, especially the executions of the
leaders, that converted public opinion. As Professor Lee has pointed out,
it was *articulate* opinion that expressed the hostility to the Rising: mainly
the Unionists and the families of those fighting in France. Unionists and
leaders of the Home Rule Irish Parliamentary Party, Redmond and Dillon,
had every reason to assert that there was little support for the men of
1916. However, Professor Lee has argued that this animosity has been
given too much significance, and that there was probably more sympathy
from Dubliners than has been hitherto thought. Furthermore, Professor
Lee has suggested that account should be taken of the lack of proper
reporting during the week, with only the *Irish Times* managing to publish,
and the other main Dublin papers failing to appear until the Rising was
over. This Unionist paper would hardly have been sympathetic to the
Rising, and on the second day, the Tuesday, the Rising was dismissed in
three lines, while the following day the edition was dominated by reports
on the annual Royal Dublin Society Show and World War I. What was
significant was the inability to ascertain what was actually going on, and
the fact there was some delay between the event and the reports in the
press, which were not generally based on first-hand knowledge – thus at
first, public opinion was being shaped by rumours and inadequate
information.[6] Thus truly contemporary accounts by Dubliners, who were

not relying totally on surmise, confused reports and second- or third-hand accounts, are a vital source to the historian. Above all, as Fannin himself stated, 'the papers will have given you a fair idea of what took place but the feelings of those who went through it must be imagined.'[7] It is these 'feelings' that are captured in the diaries of 1916. Also, no one person's expectations and experiences were the same, and thus, as Professor R.F. Foster suggested, there is a need to examine as many diaries of the Rising as possible in order to establish an overall picture.[8]

Alfred Fannin's diary is a first-hand account, written at the time, as the Rising was unfolding, though some of the early comments, particularly, were based on rumour and information from others. Above all it was not written for publication, but was a private letter to his brother, as he stressed in the final words of his letter of 6 May: 'the notes . . . are only for your own reading and you will make allowances for the point of view taken'. It is, however, only one person's view, and Fannin himself recognized this limitation when at the end of the account he comments that on reading through the notes 'they seem unduly introspective'.[9] His observations are geographically confined to his own sphere, the Southern part of the city, where he both lived and worked; he did not venture North of the river during Easter Week, and it is curious that there is no mention in the diary of the burning of Sackville Street and the destruction of that part of Dublin, which was likened to scenes from towns on the battlefront in Europe – 'a Louvain by the Liffey'.[10] The social perspective is a restricted one, for this is an account of a well-to-do middle-class family, and there are no comments on the views of the servants or less well-off sections of society. From a gender point of view, the observations are made from the male position, but they do give a little insight into the response of and attitudes to the women in the family, how his wife, Violet, was nervous of the fighting coming near to their home, and of Alfred's decision to conceal from them his narrow escape from snipers' bullets and the closeness of the fighting.[11] Fannin's wry amusement at having to do the shopping is also revealing:

> I am sure you would smile to see the long lines of people carrying home loaves of bread across the Park from Johnston Mooney's (myself amongst them) or to see your humble servant with an armful of cauliflower returning from Upper Leeson Street.[12]

Such information highlights the social (albeit temporary!) effects of the Rising as, for the first time in their lives, better-off men stepped out of their normal role and position in society.

32 Herbert Park, the Fannin residence.

Fannin's of Grafton St (supplied by the *Irish Times*).

The Fannins lived in a select area in South Dublin; in 1912 they had moved into No. 32, Herbert Park, for which they paid £1200 and which had been built according to Mrs Violet Fannin's specifications. The street – a new development – offered comfortable and substantial homes. Their's was one of the finer houses in Herbert Park, and in 1916 had the second highest rateable value. Neighbours included some well-known figures, Eoin MacNeill, The O'Rahilly, F.H. Browning and the director of Jameson's Distillery, Arthur Mitchell – some of whom were to play a key role in the events of 1916; most of the occupiers in the street were professional men: lawyers, doctors, academics etc.[13] Herbert Park, however, was close to the centre and to some of the fighting, and this makes the Fannin diary a useful source.[14]

The diary particularly reflects the response of commerce to the Rising, for Alfred Fannin was managing director of Fannin and Co., a medical supplies firm which still bears the name,[15] and which until fairly recently occupied the same premises at 41 Grafton Street, that Alfred Fannin strove to reach during the Rising. In 1916 this was a major company which had, in effect, a monopoly in supplying Ireland's hospitals. The business had been founded in 1829 by Alfred's great grandfather, Thomas Fannin, and was passed down to his son and then his grandson, Alfred's father, Thomas Eustace, who died in 1888, when Alfred and his brother Edward were still in their mid-teens.[16] Edward, the elder brother, chose not to make his career in the firm; instead he trained as a medical practitioner, and in World War I volunteered for active service as a doctor. He did not, however, sever his links with Fannin's, and remained as a 'sleeping' director, becoming chairman in 1930. It was thus Alfred who ran the business, having taken an Arts degree at Trinity College Dublin. On his death in 1939 it was passed to his only son Eustace, who managed it until it was sold in the mid-1970s. There was one other member in the family who was closely associated with the firm: Richard Booth, Alfred and Edward's uncle, to whom they turned for guidance after their father's death. Richard Booth, an entrepreneur and head of an engineering firm, was himself a prominent member of Dublin's business world;[17] and at the time of the Rising was also a director of the Dublin and South Eastern Railway, a Justice of the Peace, and President of the Dublin Chamber of Commerce. Alfred Fannin's overriding concern was for the fortunes of his business, and there are a number of places in his correspondence with his brother where this is quite apparent. Almost the last words of his follow-up letter of 10 May bemoan the fact that he lost a fortnight's trade because of the Rising, and, in addition to this loss, he had still ensured that the staff received their full wages.[18] It was concern for commerce that prompted many involved in business to sign a mass petition to Prime Minister Asquith (one of these signatories being Alfred Fannin), which called for the continuance of martial law. The Dublin Chamber of Commerce likewise passed a similar resolution.[19]

The *Irish Times* obituary notice for Alfred Fannin on his death in late 1939 emphasized the amount of charitable work he had done in his life.[20] Not only had he been a shrewd businessman, but he had been closely involved with the Methodist Church and its associated activities. The Fannin, Booth, Crawford and Parsons families, who were all closely related by marriage, were all leading Methodist families, and it could be suggested that the diary gives an insight into how members of this close religious and social community responded to the Rising.[21] Their church, the Centenary Church, was an imposing classically-fronted stone building in St Stephen's Green, and was very close to key positions taken by the insurgents. Thus Alfred Fannin would have particular reason to be anxious. What is also interesting is the paramount role of Methodism in their lives – Richard Booth still insisted on attending the Annual Wesleyan Missionary Society meeting in London at the end of Easter Week.[22] Irish Methodists had generally been Unionist in their sympathies and, in 1886, at the time of the first Irish Home Rule Bill, their Conference had endorsed with an overwhelming majority a petition that no measure should be supported which might lead to Ireland's legislative independence. However, support for Home Rule did grow a little among Methodists, as the voting revealed at their Conference in 1914, when the third Home Rule Bill was passing into law. One committed Home Rule nationalist was Alfred Fannin's uncle, William Crawford, a major figure among Dublin Methodists, who from 1899 to 1910 had been principal of Wesley College (situated next door to the Centenary Church);[23] but there is no evidence of the Fannins' views on their uncle's opinions.

In 1912 William Crawford published an article, 'The Methodist Church in Ireland', in which he argued convincingly for Home Rule. The wishes of democracy must prevail, he wrote, and he was very critical of the Ulster Unionists for attempting to impose their wishes on three-quarters of the Irish population. One of the key messages of his article was the need for a mood of toleration and conciliation, and it was particularly incumbent on Irish Protestants to show good will: 'Thus Protestantism may yet be enabled to make some pious reparation for many an unholy deed done in her name to the most generous people under the sun.' Crawford stressed how Protestants and Catholics had been able to work together in charitable work and the 'area of social amenities', while a Home Rule parliament would not threaten true Protestant interests, for example, education, temperance, Sunday observance, marriage laws and morals – these were clearly the sentiments of a Methodist. England must recognize Ireland's right to nationality, but in line with most Irish nationalists at this time he believed that Ireland should have self-government, 'so far as it is compatible with the interests of the Empire, to which Ireland belongs and must still belong unless a mighty convulsion of nature puts it elsewhere'.[24]

The Fannins were thrifty and private people; social contacts revolved round their family and the Methodist Centenary Church, and this comes across in the diary.[25] Alfred Fannin did not record conversations and contacts with people he did not know; his behaviour did not accord with the description James Stephens gave of the Rising's impact on Dubliners' social conduct:

> Meanwhile the sun was shining ... In the streets of Dublin there were no morose faces to be seen. Almost everyone was smiling and attentive, and a democratic feeling was abroad, to which our city is very much a stranger; for while in private we are a social and talkative people, we have no street manners or public ease whatever. Every person spoke to every other person, and men and women mixed without constraint.[26]

However, in addition to Methodism and commerce, the diary also gives some insight into the impact on Dublin's medical world. The *Irish Times* commented on how the hospitals still managed despite the fact that their resources were severely stretched, and praised the 'doctors and nurses [who] were almost in the thick of the fighting, and risked their lives many times a day with magnificent audacity.' The Royal City of Dublin Hospital's board of directors gave particular thanks to their doctors during the Rising, for the hospital had handled more than two hundred casualties; Dr Alfred Parsons, Alfred Fannin's brother-in-law, who played a prominent part in the diary, was one of the names singled out for mention. Alfred Parsons was a leading Dublin doctor, and included J.M. Synge among his patients. It is also worthy of mention that he gave evidence for the defence of Captain Bowen-Colthurst at his court-martial for the murder of Francis Sheehy-Skeffington and others. Dr Parsons argued that 'his condition was far from normal and that he was unbalanced', and he suggested that this had been first brought on by the intense strain of fighting at the Front in the war.[27]

Alfred Fannin and Dr Parsons, because they were in the medical world, were allowed more mobility than most Dubliners, though even so there were restrictions on their movements. However, such relative freedom does give more credence to Fannin's account. His diary gives information on the food shortages, looting, the role of rumour, the element of surprise when the Rising began, and the military aspects – though it also reflects the confusion about what was happening and who planned it. Fannin observed the events of Easter week with a certain amount of restraint. He did not see it as a spectacle, unlike 'J.J.' O'Leary (later a prominent printer) who told his story in the *Dublin Saturday Post*, and who seemed quite exhilarated with the whole experience; his rather graphic descriptions seized on the 'magnificent scenes' of the fires, on the 'brilliancy . . . and grandeur of the spectacle'.[28] Fannin's response was calm and he concentrated on going about his work as much as possible, and getting much-needed supplies moving. It is also interesting that Fannin did not condemn the Rising outright; he did not express hostility or call for the leaders to be punished. He simply reported on the fact a member of his staff in the shop was a 'Sinn Feiner' and was killed in the Rising: there is no horror, but also no secret admiration for their courage. His tone of detachment, however, was not so absolute as Stephens had observed among Dubliners:

> I received the impression that numbers of them did not care a rap what way it went; and that others had ceased to be mental creatures and were merely machines for registering the sensations of the time. None of these people were prepared for Insurrection. The thing had been sprung on them so suddenly that they were unable to take sides, and their feeling of detachment was still so complete that they would have betted on the business as if it had been a horse race or a dog fight.[29]

There are a few hints of Fannin's attitude: his use of the term 'rebels'; the hope for the arrival of heavy guns, the response to the British troops and the concern over the casualties they sustained, the reference to 'we' which identifies himself with the British Empire – as indeed did the leader of

the Irish Parliamentary Party, John Redmond. There is no suggestion
that the executions had had any impact on his attitude – here again, they
are just reported in a detached manner.[30]

What is particularly striking in the diary, however, is the longing for
a return to normality, and the sense of relief as the end came into sight.
Like John Dillon in his account, Alfred Fannin expressed the sense of
isolation that Dubliners had felt. But perhaps the main psychological
effect of the Rising on Dubliners for the Fannins was the interruption it
presented to the course of their everyday lives. On Monday 1 May, Alfred
wrote, in what for him were less restrained and more moving terms:

> At ordinary times we hate the chiming of St Bartholomew's every
> quarter hour and its out-of-tune hymn tunes at intervals.
> Throughout this week we have felt it the one thing permanent
> and regular apart of course from the forces of Nature and the work
> of God.[31]

1   See below, p. 19.
2   Mrs Arthur Mitchell to her sister Flora, 24–27 April 1916, NLI, MS 24553.
3   J. Stephens, *The Insurrection in Dublin*, ed. Michael Adams (Dublin, 1965), pp. 37–8; John Dillon to Lady Mathew, 25 April – 1 May 1916, John Dillon Papers, TCD MS 9820; Mrs Arthur Mitchell to her sister, 24–27 April 1916, NLI, MS 24553; examples of contemporary (or near-contemporary) accounts are: at TCD: R.A. Tweedy (of Killiney) to his mother, 7 May 1916, MS 7533/3–4; Douglas Hyde, 'Reflections after Easter Week', Nellie O'Brien Papers, MS 10343/7; Elsie Mahaffy (the Provost's daughter), 'Ireland in 1916 – an account of the rising in Dublin', MS 2074; in NLI: Thomas King Moylan, 'A Dubliner's Diary, 1914 - 1918', MS 9620; John Clarke's diary (a Catholic shopkeeper), MS 10485; William G. Smith's account (a St John's Ambulance volunteer), 24 June 1916, MS 24952; Monk Gibbon's record written from contemporary notes, MS 5808.
4   See below, pp. 19–20, note 25.
5   J. Lee, *Ireland, 1912–1985, politics and society* (Cambridge, 1989), pp. 24–6.
6   J. Lee, *Ireland, 1912–1985*, pp. 24–38; *Irish Times*, 25, 26 April 1916; see also, J. Stephens, *Insurrection in Dublin*, pp. 27, 36–7.
7   See below, p. 47.
8   Stated during the discussion of Professor C. Townshend's paper on the Rising delivered at Hertford College, Oxford, 5 November 1992.
9   See below, p. 45.
10 Deputation to the Home Secretary from the Corporation of Dublin headed by the Lord Mayor made shortly after the Rising (Asquith Papers, Bodleian, MS 44, f. 61).
11 See below, pp. 21, 28–9, 31–3.

12 See below, p. 44.
13 No. 32, Herbert Park was home to Alfred Fannin's son Eustace until his death in 1985, and is now an ambassadorial residence. See below, pp. 16, 19, notes 10 and 23 for further details on some of these names.
14 E.g. at the Ballsbridge end of Herbert Park, Beggars Bush Barracks, and the Haddington Road, Northumberland Road and Pembroke Road area. See map.
15 Now 'Fannin Healthcare'.
16 See family tree.
17 Richard Wilson Booth had, with his brother, founded the family tool retail business, which turned to selling bicycles. He seized the opportunity offered by Mr Dunlop's invention of pneumatic tyres to form a highly successful company which eventually became the Dunlop Rubber Company.
18 See below, pp. 21–2, 35, 51.
19 Memorial to Asquith, signed by 763 persons in Dublin, Cork, etc. 12–15 May 1916; Chamber of Commerce resolution, 15 May 1916 (Asquith papers, Bodleian, MS 42, ff. 90–137; MS 36, f. 196).
20 *Irish Times*, 1 Jan. 1940.
21 See below, pp. 27–8, and note 54. A useful source for details on Dublin Methodists is the publication, *Methodist Centenary Church, St Stephens Green. A commemorative record* (Dublin, 1943), to which Alfred Fannin contributed a chapter.
22 See below, p. 38.
23 F. Jeffery, *Methodism and the Irish problem* (Belfast, 1973), pp. 28–9.
24 W. Crawford, 'The Methodist Church in Ireland', in *The new Irish Constitution*, edited on behalf of the Eighty Club by J.H. Morgan (London, 1912), pp. 472–91.
25 Alfred Fannin's visits to the homes of Mr Harte and Dr Irwin and his stopping to chat with the church organist Alfie Deale, see below, pp. 28, 31.
26 J. Stephens, *Insurrection in Dublin*, pp. 37.
27 *Weekly Irish Times, Sinn Fein Rebellion Handbook* (1917), pp. 20, 107–10, 233–4.
28 *Dublin Saturday Post*, one edition covering 29 April, 6, 13 May 1916.
29 J. Stephens, *Insurrection in Dublin*, pp. 52–3.
30 See below, pp. 23–4, 33, 42–3, 47–9.
31 See below, p. 43.

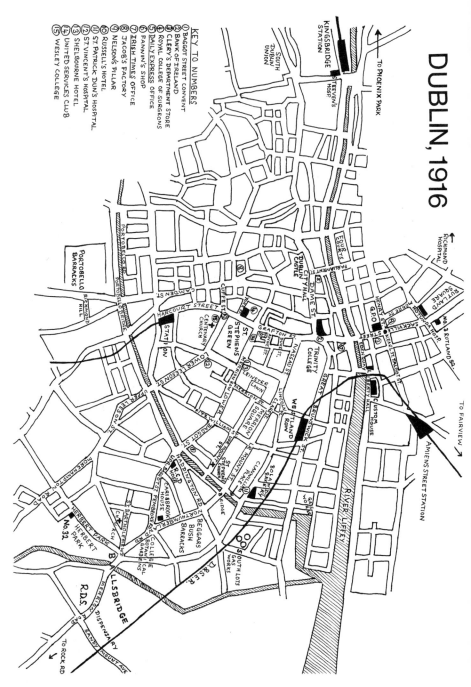

Map of Dublin in 1916 – Places mentioned in the 'Diary' (By A. Warwick-Haller).

Dear Ed

It is 10.30 A.M. Easter Tuesday morning and I have not gone in to business. I am detained at home with nothing to do and sit down to write some account of what happened yesterday in Dublin.

We had planned for golf at Greystones[1] and at 10 yesterday morning. Emma[2] & Helen Crawford,[3] Alfie[4] and I in Alfie's motor. We were to meet Edwin and Edith [Booth][5] at Greystones. Their car broke down and they did not get down till lunch time. I played a single with Helen, and in the afternoon, Emma and Alf played a single again & Helen and I played Edith and Ed. At lunch time one of the men at the clubhouse tried to telephone to town but was told that the wire into town was cut,[6] that the Sinn Feiners[7] were

1   Greystones was a fashionable coastal resort about 20 miles south of Dublin.
2   Emma Parsons was the author's sister-in-law. She acted as 'housekeeper' to her brother, Dr Alfred Parsons.
3   Helen Crawford was a member of a Dublin Methodist family, and Alfred and Edward Fannin's first cousin; her father was the Reverend William Crawford, principal of Wesley College, 1899–1910. See above, introduction, pp. 7–8, and see family tree.
4   Dr Alfred Parsons was often called 'Balfour' to distinguish him from Alfred Fannin. He was a Senior Consultant Physician at the Royal City of Dublin Hospital, Baggot Street. He was the author's brother-in-law.
5   Edwin and Edith Booth were husband and wife. Edwin was a first cousin of the author – his father, Richard Booth, being Edward and Alfred Fannin's uncle. (See family tree.)
6   One of the early moves of the insurgents' plan was to disrupt communications by cutting telephone and telegraph links, thereby delaying the authorities' ability to request assistance and military reinforcements. They were only partly successful in destroying these links. (See Col. P.J. Hally, 'The Easter 1916 Rising in Dublin: the military aspects', part 2, in the *Irish Sword*, viii, no. 30 [Summer 1967], pp. 54–5).
7   Other contemporary accounts, Dubliners, the British authorities, the press, all

out and had occupied Westland Row Station.[8] Although there had been some rumours[9] during the week of trouble with the S.Fs no one had thought there was anything in it. Balfour and Emma played 9 holes after lunch and started for town about 4 o'clock, reaching

mistakenly described the insurgents as 'Sinn Feiners', and the Rising as a 'Sinn Fein Rising'. Alfred Fannin himself used the title 'April 1916 Rising of Sinn Fein' on the brown manila folder in which the diary was kept. Before the Rising, Sinn Fein (translated 'Ourselves' or 'Our Own Thing') was in fact the name of Arthur Griffith's movement, which sought Ireland's independence from Britain through political, economic and cultural self-sufficiency. Sinn Fein, as it was originally conceived, was a movement that advocated passive resistance rather than physical force; moreover, by 1916 it had been in decline for some years. The Rising was actually the work of the small and secret Military Council of the Irish Republican Brotherhood, and was carried out by a breakaway group (of about 1600) of the Irish Volunteers and James Connolly's 200-strong Irish Citizen Army. Griffith (and Sinn Fein) had not been involved in planning '1916', nor did he take part, though he had offered his services during the course of the week, but had been told his main duty was to preserve his life for Ireland's future. As relatively little was known about the real leaders of the Rising and their intentions, the only description readily available to observers like Alfred Fannin was that of 'Sinn Fein', of which there was a much greater public awareness, and which had had a strong influence on advanced nationalist thinking. Later in the diary Fannin did on one occasion refer to 'volunteers' (see below, p. 40).

8   Westland Row was a main railway station of strategic importance. It was part of the insurgents' plan to occupy the stations to prevent British reinforcements being brought in. The *Irish Times* reported that Westland Row and Harcourt Street stations were quickly seized, and the rails on the Kingstown line were attacked, but Harcourt Street station was found unsuitable for defence, and was abandoned within a few hours (*Irish Times*, 25 April 1916). Westland Row, however, remained occupied until 3 May.

9   Rumours that some kind of action against the British was being planned had been circulating in Ireland for several months. Extreme nationalists had been publicly proclaiming that Ireland must take action before the end of the war, and that men must be prepared to sacrifice themselves for Ireland. The week before the Rising, however, certain incidents had suggested that something was afoot: the publication of the so-called 'Castle Document', which pointed to the fact that the Government anticipated and was trying to forestall an insurrection (though it was swiftly denounced as a forgery it would have added to the 'rumours'); the interception by British warships of the *Aud*, the German ship bringing arms; the arrest of Roger Casement as he landed from a German submarine. Above all, the eleventh hour attempt to stop the Rising made by the head of the Volunteers, Eoin MacNeill, and his orders countermanding the planned manoeuvres that Sunday (the day when the Rising was originally scheduled to start), helped to ensure that the Rising was largely a Dublin affair.

FAMILY TREE

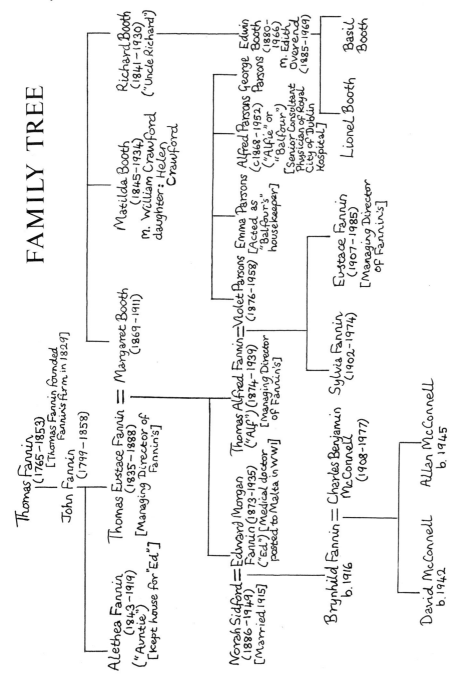

Fannin family tree.

town about 5 P.M. They came to Herbert Park[10] and heard that Violet[11] & her mother had heard shots during the day and vague rumours also that Eustace's[12] Nan [nanny][13] who had been up from the country to pay him a visit could not get to Kingsbridge[14] but had been turned back at the Four Courts by men who were firing out of it.[15] Balfour then went to [the] hospital[16] and found that there were some serious casualties there. About 5 o'clock in the afternoon a number of G.Rs (the football corps organised by Mr Browning our neighbour) were returning to Beggars Bush Barracks from a route march carrying rifles but no ammunition. As they reached the corner where Haddington Road intersects Northumberland Road they were fired on at point blank range by a number of Sinn Feiners who had seized one of the corner houses. Several were shot down at once, others escaped by getting into houses or making off.[17] Balfour picked up one in his car who was shot through the lungs and who only lived about half an hour after reaching hospi-

10   The author and his family lived at No. 32, Herbert Park, Ballsbridge, South Dublin. Herbert Park had also been the home of two leading Irish Nationalists: At No. 19 was Eoin MacNeill, the famed Gaelic scholar and titular head of the Irish Volunteers, who by April 1916 was living in Rathfarnham, and at No. 40, The O'Rahilly, a leading member of the Gaelic League. The latter had taken part in the Howth gun-running in 1914, but had opposed the Rising and had helped MacNeill in his attempt to prevent it. The O'Rahilly, however, joined the insurgents in the G.P.O., and was killed later in the week. He drove out from Herbert Park to take part in the Rising in his fine De Dion Bouton car, which was later found burnt out.
11   Violet Fannin (*née* Parsons, sister of Emma and Alfred Parsons).
12   Eustace was the author's son, aged nine years – see introduction, pp. 1, 6.
13   Nan almost certainly refers to Eustace's nanny. His grandmother on his father's side had died in 1911 – see family tree.
14   Kingsbridge station was another key railway station, but the insurgents failed in their attempt to take it.
15   The Four Courts, the famous porticoed and high-domed building on the river which housed the law courts, was of strategic importance to the insurgents; it was occupied early on in the Rising and men were posted throughout the building to attack troops coming along the quays from the direction of Phoenix Park.
16   Presumably the Royal City of Dublin Hospital.
17   The G.Rs (Georgius Rex) were a part-time volunteer veteran corps, a home defence force composed of old rugby club members, ex-British army soldiers and business and professional men, and were based at Beggars Bush Barracks and Kingstown. They had originally paraded in civilian clothes with armbands bear-

tal.[18] He sent his car back for others and settled down to do the work of the Surgical Staff. Johnson[19] was at Fairyhouse[20] & Stoney[21] at Greystones so he had to carry on with the resident staff till the Surgeons came back. Some of the wounds he said were ghastly.

ing the G.R. insignia, but after formal recognition wore khaki uniforms with 'Georgius Rex' on their belts. The majority being elderly, the force was affectionately and irreverently referred to by Dubliners as 'the Gorgeous Wrecks'. The incident referred to here was one of the early actions of the Rising. The G.Rs had been out on a field day in the Dublin mountains south of the city when they heard the news of the Rising. According to one account, the information that they received had led them to conclude that the fighting was in the centre of the city and away from the direction of their barracks. As Fannin correctly records, they were carrying rifles but no ammunition. The batallion had been divided into two parts for the field manoeuvres and they took separate routes back to the barracks. The larger section, under Major Harris of Trinity College O.T.C., though coming under some fire, had managed to reach the security of the barracks. But it was the smaller group (of about forty men) under F.H. Browning's command that had taken the route back that brought them on to Northumberland Road where they were fired on at close range. Five were killed and eight wounded, Browning himself fatally so. Once it was realized that the G.Rs were unable to return fire and were, in effect, unarmed, the insurgents immediately ceased firing, and the incident was regretted once the full facts were understood. Moreover, when it became known in the city that a group of elderly and defenceless men had been shot down public reaction against the 'Sinn Feiners' was very hostile. That evening Pearse was forced to give an order prohibiting firing on anyone not carrying weapons – whether or not they were in uniform. (For accounts see: M. Caulfield, *The Easter Rebellion* [London, 1965], pp. 133-5; C.St L. Duff, *Six days to shake an empire* [London, 1966], pp. 132-3; and an eye-witness account by Henry Hanna, a member of the G.Rs, TCD, MS 10066/192.)

18   Max Caulfield in his book on the Rising quotes a contemporary account of the attack on the G.Rs on Northumberland Road and the tending of the wounded from a woman who lived in the area: 'I return again to the window just in time to see a bare-headed white-coated doctor drive up in a motor-car. He disappears into one of the houses where he tends the wounded, some of whom are carried off to the hospital' (*The Easter Rebellion*, p. 134). That doctor could well have been Balfour, or certainly one of his colleagues. Many of the dead and wounded were taken to the R.C.D. Hospital, and the doctors and others who helped would have been at considerable risk in going to their aid under cross fire.

19   Johnson – probably George Jameson Johnston, surgeon and lecturer in clinical surgery at the Royal City of Dublin Hospital. See p. 36 below.

20   Fairyhouse racecourse. The race meeting at Fairyhouse, Co. Meath, north-east of Dublin, was an important Easter occasion. Many of the officers and troops protecting Dublin Castle were on leave at this meeting, leaving the Castle virtually undefended.

21   Richard Atkinson Stoney, a surgeon at the Royal City of Dublin Hospital.

The Fannin family at 32 Herbert Park (summer 1915); Alfred and Violet Fannin, their daughter Sylvia and son Eustace; on right, Edward Fannin and his fiancée, Nora Sidford.

One man had a hole in the back of his popliteal space [behind the knee] that you could put your hand into. He will lose his leg and almost his life. [Author's marginal note: Later – many bullets were doctored.][22] Up to this morning in Baggot St. [Hospital] there have been three deaths. F.H. Browning who lives opposite me and who was at the head of the column is seriously wounded.[23] There has been nothing in Dublin like this in our generation.[24]

About 12 o'clock in the day, Easter Monday, the Sinn Feiners had tried to occupy all the Railway stations – some successfully, others not, the G.P.O., Jacob's factory and other places, and Stephen's Green, barricaded all the doors, fired on anyone in uniform who approached.[25] They have blocked the streets nearing Stephen's

22 It is not perhaps entirely clear here whether Fannin is referring to the treatment and removal of bullets or that bullets had been tampered with to make them more damaging on impact. The context makes the latter meaning seem the more likely. Sean O'Casey in his play about the Rising, *The plough and the stars*, suggested that dum-dum bullets (soft-nosed expanding bullets) were used by the insurgents. A lawyer, Henry Hanna, who was also a member of the G.Rs, noted that medical examination of G.Rs who were killed revealed a variety of ammunition including dum-dums, and a number of other contemporary accounts would substantiate this view (H. Hanna's account, TCD, MS 10066/192; Monk Gibbon's record, NLI, MS 5808; *Sinn Fein Rebellion Handbook*, published by the *Weekly Irish Times*, 1917, pp. 14, 19, 171). On the other hand, however, an article in a recent book on the Rising has dismissed O'Casey's claim, and has stated that a British inquiry found no evidence that dum-dum bullets had been used (D. Kiberd, 'The elephant of revolutionary forgetfulness', in M. Ni Dhonnchadha & T. Dorgan [eds], *Revising the Rising* [Derry, 1991], p. 18).

23 He later died. (See below, p. 33) F.H. Browning (mistakenly written by Fannin as J.H. . . .), a graduate of Trinity College Dublin, and affectionately known as 'Chicken' Browning to his friends, had been an outstanding cricketer, and was also a keen follower of rugby football, having been president of Irish Rugby Union when war broke out. He had been responsible for forming the Irish Rugby Volunteer Corps. A detailed obituary appeared in the *Irish Times* of 2 May 1916.

24 The last time Dublin – or indeed Ireland – was affected by an insurrection was during the abortive Fenian rising of 1867, when the insurgents, instead of acting inside the city, marched into the snow-covered Dublin mountains. In comparison with 1867, or its predecessors, 1848 and 1798, 1916 did have some kind of coherent military plan.

25 The insurgents' plan for the rising in Dublin was to take over strategic places in the centre which would give them a controlling position over army barracks and routes into the city. Some of the points chosen were very appropriate, but would

Green, and while they allow civilians to walk about are shooting at anyone they see in Khaki.

Throughout the night we heard a good deal of firing, mostly rifles.

The news this Tuesday morning is that the soldiers have retaken the Castle,[26] are marching on Stephen's Green and then are to take Westland Row. Of course everything is rumour and surmise.[27] But if it is true that the military are on the move the whole thing will be cleared up very soon. On the other hand, street fighting in Dublin with modern rifles will be a very serious matter.[28]

Both Balfour and Violet say it is madness to attempt to get into town as the fighting is at present going on in Stephen's Green and one would only be turned back.

have required much larger numbers to provide proper military strength. The plan also contained some strategic weaknesses: there was no provision to take Dublin Castle and Trinity College. It could be argued that Trinity would have provided a better headquarters than the G.P.O.: from its central position it could have helped the Volunteers in St Stephen's Green and in Jacob's Biscuit Factory; it would have been easier to defend; and the British authorities might very well have been reluctant to shell it and destroy its fine buildings and put at risk its priceless collections of books and manuscripts. The G.P.O. may have had some advantages, but it could be easily encircled and cut off from the rest of the city. Michael Collins (who was in the G.P.O.) wrote some six months later that the Rising was 'bungled terribly, costing many a good life. It seemed at first to be well organized, but afterwards became subjected to panic decisions and a great lack of very essential organization and co-operation' (see F.X. Martin, 'The 1916 Rising – a *Coup d'etat* or a "bloody protest"?'– p. 131 for Collins' words), and P.J. Hally, 'The Easter 1916 Rising in Dublin: the military aspects' – full details in Bibliography); see also note 33 below.

26 Dublin Castle was the seat of British authority in Ireland. The garrison had, in fact, been greatly reduced because a lot of the men were away on leave, many having gone to the Fairyhouse races. One of the first moves the insurgents made was to attack the Castle, and it could easily have been taken on that Easter Monday; but the insurgents were not aware of that, and occupying it was, apparently, not part of their overall plan.

27 The lack of proper communications helped to foster the rumours that spread through Dublin; other accounts, James Stephens', for example, are full of rumours, and some of those Stephens reported are also in Fannin's account. See pp. 42–3.

28 Given the overwhelming odds against them, the insurgents could not have hoped for military success, and the general view is that the leaders, especially Pearse, were

The sentries at the Castle and the Bank of Ireland were shot dead yesterday.

Mrs Travers Smith[29] told Nan yesterday that she saw a driver of a lorry shot dead near the Shelbourne because he refused to give up his lorry, it was three times demanded and then they shot him.[30]

We are well here but of course Violet's nerves are a bit on the go and the whole thing has absolutely to be kept from Ewie [Eustace]. A rather hard thing when he can hear the firing just as plainly as we can. He has to be told it is only practice.

Later, 8 P.M., April 25th

I did not go into town this morning on Alfie's advice and on account of Violet's anxiety. Smith came to see me about 12 o'clock.

driven by the image of their 'blood sacrifice': that martyrdom would eventually produce an independent Ireland. The Rising only lasted a week, but that was a long time for them to hold out. This interpretation of the Rising – that it was envisaged as a blood-sacrifice – has been questioned. (See above, introduction, pp. 2–3.) The immediate effects on Dubliners, however, would last longer than a week, with the drawn-out executions of the leaders and the imposition of martial law. History was, of course, to prove Alfred Fannin wrong in his hope that 'the whole thing will be cleared up very soon', but right in his perception of the consequences of street fighting with modern weapons.

29 Mrs Travers Smith probably represented another connection with Dublin's medical world – there was an R. Travers Smith M.D. of Fitzwilliam Square.

30 The Shelbourne was a major hotel on St Stephen's Green. It was frequented by the Anglo-Irish ascendancy. The hotel was only temporarily occupied by the insurgents, and it would have been a good building to seize because of its height (it was the tallest building in the area). British troops subsequently took it over, and were then in a good position to counter the insurgents in the College of Surgeons, also on the Green. James Connolly, when taking his Citizen Army on a march round the city some weeks before the Rising to reconnoitre the key strategic sites, had indicated that the Shelbourne would make a suitable barracks with a plentiful supply of food and beds. The story of the man with a lorry-cart who was shot is told at length and more graphically in two accounts: by James Stephens, *Insurrection in Dublin*, ed. Michael Adams (Dublin, 1965) pp. 24–5; and by a St John's Ambulance volunteer who commented on how awful the effect was on the crowd, and how he himself was greatly shocked by what he had witnessed: William G. Smith, 24 June 1916, NLI, MS 24952.

He had gone in and opened the shop as usual.[31] All our people were in except one man in the workshop who is reputed a Sinn Feiner. [Author's marginal note: Later. He was, and was brought in dead to Steven's Hospital.] There was no business to be done except so far as the Hospitals rang up for stuff. We cannot originate calls. The telephones being reserved for Military calls only. Some surgical dressings required for the Richmond Hospital were sent out. The messengers had to get permits from the Sinn Fs to get through the barricades in Sackville St. [now O'Connell Street]. Very little business was to be done so he closed after a couple of hours. None of our people had any difficulty in getting to or from business although shooting was going on in Stephen's Green. A great deal of the shooting is aimless. There is a barricade of Motor Cars across the road opposite Russell's Hotel, another near York Street.[32] The College of Surgeons is held by the rebels with a republican flag over it. Kenny saw a man shot in Lr Leeson Street while on his way into town.

Several houses in Lr Leeson St were occupied by S.Fs during the night and given up in the morning. It is not easy to see much at Stephen's Green. It is said there are only about 1 doz. S.Fs at each

31   No. 41, Grafton Street – the Fannins' surgical instruments and appliances business
      (see above, introduction, pp. 6–7).
32   James Stephens' account and J.R. Clegg's 'A Citizen's Diary' in the *Irish Times*
      also tell of barricades of motor-cars and carts across the streets in this area; cars
      were being commandeered by the insurgents, and their occupants required to leave
      them. (See below, p. 25.) Lionel Booth has recounted a story about his grandfather,
      Richard Booth, who was Alfred Fannin's uncle. As a director of the Dublin and
      South Eastern Railway Company, Richard Booth, on hearing that his head office
      at Westland Row had been occupied, decided that some valuable documents must
      be retrieved from a safe in that office. He wisely chose to take a horse and trap
      rather than a car, and he apparently sailed through or round the barricades and
      gained access to the Westland Row office through a door under the railway bridge
      for which he had a key. There he was greeted cheerfully by the insurgents, and was
      allowed to take whatever he wanted from the safe and drive home without en-
      countering any trouble. To cite Lionel's words: 'Somehow that generation seem
      to have decided that a mere Rebellion must not be allowed to disturb their normal
      pattern of life.' (We are indebted to Lionel Booth for this information.)

corner in view, that their trenches are shallow and little use for protection,[33] that many are leaving the Green and taking up positions in the houses round or perhaps deserting. Short of a German invasion of England at the same time on a big scale the whole thing was doomed to failure.[34] At the same time after 36 hours rebellion, the rebels hold nearly all the points they have taken. The *Daily Express* office has been retaken by the Military, also the South Dublin Union.[35] The Bank of Ireland and the Telephone buildings are also strongly held by us. Kingsbridge was never lost and Amiens St is held by troops from Dundalk, but in the one case the 'line is reported torn up outside Dublin and in the other the railway bridge

33   The occupation of St Stephen's Green has puzzled historians; Colonel Hally has commented that from 'a military point of view' this part of the plan 'always mystified' him: surely it would have been more sensible, Hally continues, to have seized the high buildings around the Green, especially the Shelbourne, before ordering defences to be dug in the Green itself (P.J. Hally, 'The Easter 1916 Rising in Dublin: the military aspects', part 1, in *The Irish Sword*, vol. vii, no. 29 [Winter 1966], pp. 320–21; see also note 25 above). The notion of urban street fighting was not entirely understood by either side, and the digging of trenches by the insurgents reflected military thinking and practices of World War I.

34   This is another comment on the hopelessness of the insurgents' attempts from a military point of view and reinforces the 'blood sacrifice' theme of the Rising. The First World War had, however, provided the occasion for the Rising under the old maxim that 'England's difficulty is Ireland's opportunity'. In fact, fears of a peace being arranged with Germany gave added impetus to leaders like Connolly and Pearse to ensure the Rising occurred before such an eventuality. Though help had been sought, Germany had been most reluctant to become involved and the most she would commit were arms. One of the rumours which circulated in Dublin held that the Rising was part of a wider plan to distract the British army while the Germans were landing. Douglas Hyde recounted that he was told this by English forces who searched his house, and he added the comment that 'This would make out the rising more dangerous and far more sane in its conception than appeared at first sight' (Douglas Hyde's diary, 'Reflections after Easter Week', 5 May 1916, Nellie O'Brien Papers, TCD, MS 10343/7). One Dublin citizen, a Robert Tweedy, wrote to his mother in London that, in his opinion the insurgents were convinced that they were taking part in a great German push by sea and land, and they had adopted defensive tactics from the beginning, gambling on a general rising of the population and, above all, German help coming before Britain could send troops from England. Tweedy added the comment: 'We call them madmen now because they did not succeed, but we shall not know for a long time how mad they really were' (R.A. Tweedy to his mother, 7 May 1916, TCD, MS 7533/3-4).

35   The latter point was incorrect; the insurgents in the South Dublin Union held out all week.

crossing the road from the Promised Land at Fairview has been reported blown up.[36] [Author's marginal note: Later on, both of these were untrue.] So that troops from North and South can reach the Suburbs at any rate. There are no artillery nearer than Athlone and it is reported these are coming by road.[37] I went as far as Lr Baggot Street this afternoon, and everything seemed quiet; but from the bridge we could hear heavier guns than any yet heard and one hoped for their arrival. Artillery could hardly travel 80 miles in a day. Some troops reached Dublin from the Curragh[38] at 6 o'clock in the morning and were paraded in Lr Fitzwilliam St (about 2000). I do not know where they were used later in the day. The Military hold the Shelbourne Hotel and a battle is going on across the road all day.[39] It is rumoured that Capt de Burgh Daly, the recruiting Medical Officer, was shot at in the U.S. [United Services] Club[40] by the Countess Markievicz[41] from the other side of the road. [This sentence is marked by the author with a line and a marginal note: Later incorrect.] It is also rumoured that Sir Roger Casement has been captured in the South and run over to England and is now in

36 In the original Alfred Fannin initially wrote 'viaduct' before 'the Promised Land' and then crossed it out. The author's niece, Brynhild McConnell, has suggested that 'the Promised Land in Fairview' was a reference to the lengthy reclamation work at the mouth of the River Tolka in North Dublin, which is now Fairview Park. She has added that this 'could have been a private "christening" of the area by the two brothers. They loved jokes.'

37 A battery of 18-pounders and the Royal Artillery Brigade were being brought up from Athlone. The guns had to come part of the way by road as the railway line from Athlone had been blown up. A Secret Operations Circular issued by Major-General F.C. Shaw (General Staff, Home Forces) at 4.20 p.m., 25 April, reported that four 18-pounder guns had left Athlone in the early hours of the morning (Asquith Papers, Bodleian, MS 42, f. 11).

38 The Curragh was the main place in Ireland where the British army was stationed.

39 See note 30 above.

40 On the North side of St Stephen's Green.

41 Constance Markievicz (*née* Gore Booth) was an officer in the Irish Citizen Army and played an active role in the Rising as second-in-command to Michael Mallin at the College of Surgeons. She was subsequently sentenced to death, but had it commuted because of her sex. Members of the Anglo-Irish community were particularly shocked to see one of their own – and a woman – taking part; for example, the account of the Rising by Elsie Mahaffy, the daughter of the Provost of Trinity College, showed no pity for the Countess (TCD, MS 2074).

the Tower.[42] Also that the German prisoners at Oldcastle have been set at liberty and that one of the barricades at the Richmond Hospital is under command of a German Officer.[43] Some troops, a Welsh Battalion has landed at Kingstown[44] and is entrenched there. Sniping went on in many parts of the city all last night and the same may be expected tonight. I have not heard of cases of civilians or men not in uniform being shot without reason but many have been shot accidentally.[45] Those who go out in Motors are ordered to give them up, if they refuse they are shot, if they give them the motors are used for barricades.[46]

42 Sir Roger Casement was a former member of the British consular service who had joined the Irish Volunteers in 1913, and had been the key figure in the abortive attempt to secure German help and to raise an Irish Brigade from prisoners of war in Germany; he had been captured a few days before the Rising on his return to Ireland – ironically on a mission to prevent the Rising from occurring because he knew it was doomed to failure. He was executed three months later.

43 This is an example of the wild rumours and fears about German involvement (see notes 27 and 34 above). John Dillon M.P., in the diary he kept during the Rising, wrote that 'many wild rumours are flying about', giving as examples reports that Germans had landed at Tralee, that German submarines were in Belfast Lough and had attacked Belfast Post Office (Dillon Papers, TCD, MS 9820). The stories of a German invasion was one of two rumours that circulated in Dublin during this time, and was certainly the favoured one. The other rumour, which does not appear in this diary, is that the Rising was bound up with a socialist revolt; this appealed particularly to William Martin Murphy of the *Irish Independent* who, as owner of the Dublin United Tramways Company, had crossed swords with Connolly during the lockout of 1913. See also J. Lee, *Ireland, 1912–1985*, p. 30.

44 Kingstown, subsequently re-named Dun Laoghaire, was the main passenger port between Dublin and the mainland.

45 It was subsequently estimated that 450 people were killed, 2614 wounded, 9 missing; of these, 132 members of the British army and the police forces were killed, and 397 wounded. The rest were civilians and insurgents. Probably the most famous civilian who died during the Rising was Francis Sheehy-Skeffington, the scholar, who had supported a number of minority causes, including women's rights and socialism. He had been a member of the Irish Citizen Army but had resigned when it became too militaristic. He was a pacifist and, while out trying to help the wounded and prevent looting on the Tuesday, 25 April, had been arrested by an Army officer, the mentally-unbalanced Bowen-Colthurst, and was 'executed', without trial the following day. (See above, introduction, pp. 8–9.)

46 See above, p. 22 and note 32.

Of course there are no posts, the *Irish Times* came out today[47] but the only news was a Proclamation by Lord Wimborne[48] and a three line notice of the Rebellion.

Wednesday, 12 noon, April 26th

So far as we heard all was quiet during the night. All of us slept well. Emma said she heard firing at 4 A.M. but it did not awake Alfie or Violet. At eight o'clock we heard several rounds of volley firing. The ladies guessed heavy guns. Alfie and I thought it was a number of rifles firing together to an order i.e. not a smattering of fire as an attack or defence. He surmised a firing party as it occurred exactly at 8 A.M.[49] There were rumours yesterday that if arms were not laid down at a certain hour no quarter would be given. After breakfast he heard from the hospital that Stephen's Green was now in the hands of the Military. Later the rumours in the road were first that

47   The *Irish Times*, a Unionist paper, was hostile to the Rising. It managed to come out during the Rising, on the 25th, 26th and 27th April, while 28th, 29th April and 1st May were put together in the one issue. It is interesting to note that the first part of the edition for Wednesday 26 April was devoted to the Royal Dublin Show – an attempt to continue as normal (see above, introduction, p. 3). The coverage of the Rising after the early days was reasonably full, and contained the odd apparently first-hand account, e.g. a day-by-day 'Citizen's Diary' by a J.R. Clegg from Rathgar, published in the *Irish Times*, 2 May 1916. The *Irish Times* subsequently produced a *Sinn Fein Rebellion Handbook*, which is a valuable primary source for historians. The offices of the other Unionist paper, the *Daily Express*, were seized by the insurgents, while the Irish Parliamentary Party suffered a severe setback during the Rising with the destruction of the premises of the leading moderate nationalist paper, the *Freeman's Journal*.
48   Lord Wimborne was the Irish Viceroy. The Rising seriously undermined the position of the civil authorities in Ireland, and Wimborne and both the Chief and Under Secretaries, Birrell and Nathan, had to resign, though Wimborne was later reinstated.
49   The ladies were right: the 'gunboat' *Helga* (or, more accurately, armed fishery protection vessel) opened fire on Liberty Hall exactly at 8.00 A.M. J.R. Clegg in his 'Citizen's Diary' of the Rising, reported in his entry for the Wednesday the comments of a witness: 'I declare to me God, the first discharge shook the bed under me, and there was no more lyin' down for me'.

the G.P.O. had been taken by the Military, second that it had not been taken. Everyone seemed to agree that Liberty Hall had been blown down by big gun fire, this was from a patrol boat coming up the river,[50] and that there was a good deal of fighting going on between Trinity College,[51] Bank of Ireland and Brunswick Street[52] held by the military and Sackville Street, G.P.O. and Parliament St, City Hall[53] held by S.Fs.

Later – Wednesday April 26th, 5 P.M.

This morning I went into town as far as Stephen's Green about 11 o'clock. I went down Leeson Street and the street there was very deserted – it was like a Sunday, there was no horse or motor traffic. The two private hospitals had white flags with a red cross up. People stood at street corners and at the windows. I had heard the houses at the foot of Lr Leeson St were in the hands of the S.Fs but saw no signs of it when I got there. Over at the railings and gate opposite Leeson St a line of carts formed a sort of barricade but I saw from the corner no sign of life in the Green. I rode down to the Centenary [Church].[54] A few people stood along close to the railings, curiosity sightseers. (As I write Balfour has rung up to say he will be detained at Hospital and may not get into Dinner. A lot of

---

50   Liberty Hall was the headquarters of Connolly's Irish Citizen Army, but at the time of the attack it was in fact unoccupied. The full-scale bombardment was particularly damaging to the insurgents' morale as it highlighted the vastly superior strength of the British forces.

51   One of the two serious mistakes that the insurgents made was not to include in their plans the taking of Trinity College: it was a natural fortress in the centre of Dublin, and as an O.T.C. centre had the added advantage of a good supply of much-needed arms and ammunition. On Easter Monday it would, like Dublin Castle, have been easy to occupy. However, TCD graduates and undergraduates were swiftly recruited to defend the college until the British troops arrived on the Wednesday; the college was then chosen to house the heaquarters of the British forces under General Maxwell – further evidence of Trinity's strategic importance. See also note 25 above.

52   Brunswick Street was renamed Pearse Street.

53   City Hall overlooked Dublin Castle.

54   The Methodist Centenary Church was situated on the south side of St Stephen's

wounded are coming in).[55] At the Centenary I saw Long who was
on the steps. I went up to the roof and looked over the Green. As
far as I could see it was quite deserted. At intervals along the railings
there were small shallow trenches dug close to the rails. A Republican Flag floated over the College of Surgeons.[56] I only saw one man
walking in the Green, he was not in uniform and was walking about
as if himself a sightseer. [Author's marginal note: Later – believe
this was Kearney who stuck to his lodge & fed the ducks through it
all.][57] A line of punctured motor cars was drawn across the road
from Russell's Hotel. The Public House at the corner of Cuffe Street
was held by the S.Fs and an occasional shot would ring out from it.
Firing also took place from the Shelbourne Hotel held by the Military. Possibly the S.Fs were out of the Green but if they were the
Military were not yet in occupation effectively. They may have
feared an ambush. While one says the Military held the Shelbourne
Hotel, it was I think a group of officers who had been reinforced by
a party with a machine gun. I went in and saw Mr Harte & Family,[58] also to Wesley College. They were all upset by the fighting
being so near but no harm had been done. Dr Irwin is still away and
only the maids were in the house.[59] I then came home. Later on,
about 12.30, I started down as far as Upper Baggot Street, but hear-
ing that fighting was beginning at Ballsbridge and the military were

Green. The Fannin and Booth families had been closely involved with the work of
this church since its beginning, and Alfred Fannin's involvement was particularly
active: throughout his life he held many offices in the various church organiza-
tions, including Secretary of the Trustees of the church; in 1916 he had been Superintendent of the Sunday School for ten years. See introduction, pp. 7–8.

55   See note 45 above.
56   Other observers also commented on the flag on the Royal College of Surgeons; for
     instance, Eileen Corrigan, a TCD student from Belfast, described it as 'quite a
     pretty one, the colours being green, white and orange. I can't understand why it
     was orange, but perhaps they call it yellow!' (*Belfast Evening Telegraph*, 5 May
     1916).
57   John Kearney was superintendent of St Stephen's Green Park; he was also a collec-
     tor at the Methodist Centenary Church. See below, p. 48.
58   Reverend F.E. Harte was the Minister of the Centenary Methodist Church.
59   Rev. T.J. Irwin was the principal of Wesley College, next door to the Centenary
     Methodist Church.

Alfred Fannin

closing the roads going South, I turned back as I had not told Violet the fighting might be so close and feared I might be cut off in Baggot St. By this time the military who had landed at Kingstown had been marching in towards town. The S.Fs had taken Carysbrook House at the junction of Pembroke Road and Northumberland Road and were to defend the road to Dublin there. Further in they held the corner of Haddington Road and Northumberland Rd and the Parochial Hall at Mount Street Bridge was another point to be defended.[60] Boland's Bakery[61] opposite Sir P. Dun's Hospital was the next line of defence. About 2 o'clock the fighting between Ballsbridge and Carysbrook House was quite brisk, the S.Fs were

60 The insurgents occupied Clanwilliam House which dominated the canal, Northumberland Road and the bridge itself. Strategically, this was a most suitable position.

61 Boland's Bakery in Grand Canal Street was one of the outposts taken by the insurgents. It was well-placed to cover the routes that British troops might take from Kingstown. De Valera was in command of the insurgents there (about 130), and he was in reality not in the actual bakery building, but in the Dispensary next door, and when the firing from the *Helga* started, he put up a flag on another building to divert attention.

Edward and Nora Fannin (November 1915).

also in the College Botanical Gardens.[62] There were several casualties. The Military remained or fell back a while behind Ballsbridge. It was dangerous at this time to go out to the far side of Herbert Park. At about 1.30 and from this [time] on a steady line of troops was passing down Morehampton Road, some small companies and some larger bodies and later we heard the artillery driving along there too. By the time I write, 5 to 6 P.M., one or two thousand must have passed by this road but I do not think many have gone through by the Rock Road. At any rate fighting is still going on there.[63] We used to think we were clear of the war here in Ireland

62   The College Botanical Gardens, at the junction of Lansdowne and Pembroke Roads, were quite close to the Fannins' home in Herbert Park.

63   This account can be reinforced by one of Alfred Fannin's neighbours, Mrs Arthur Mitchell, of No. 18, Herbert Park, who also wrote a day-by-day letter about the Rising. She, like the Fannins, was afraid to venture out on the Wednesday afternoon, but towards evening she and her sister paid a brief visit to the bottom of Herbert Park to see where the firing was coming from. 'Well it was awful', she wrote; and her sister saw what she thought were dead and wounded lying in the road. They found it hard to comprehend that there was such 'a deadly fight' going on so near their home, 'and crowds looking on as if [at] a sham battle. Whole

but we have certainly got it close enough now.[64] Nan (who can't get back yet to her place in Mountmellick) and Joan have just come in from Rathmines. They say the soldiers are holding Portobello Bridge (they have held the barracks and neighbourhood all through) and a fight is going on down Camden Street from there.

Thursday morning 9.30, April 27th

I was out later in the afternoon yesterday and heard that Carysbrook House had been taken by the Military and some casualties. Many people had been standing round Ballsbridge while it was being taken and saw the fighting close. I did not go to Ballsbridge till it was over about 6/7 P.M. but even then as I stood on the open road one bullet ricocheted off the roofs of the houses beside me and another hit the tramway wires over my head. I was chatting with Alfie Deale at the time.[65] He was home from the front and in mufti. He said it was dangerous so we walked back across the Park.[66] He had watched the fighting during the afternoon but though he had seen close fight-

families: Father, Mother, swarms of kids, pram with the baby and dog on a string which was a common sight.' These comments emphasize the almost surreal nature of the Rising for the residents of a normally quiet suburb of South Dublin (Mrs Arthur C. Mitchell's letter to her sister, Flora, 24 – 27 April 1916, NLI, MS 24553); all reasonable effort has been made to trace the owner of this diary.

64   There had initially been no shortage of Irish recruits to fight for Britain in the First World War; Redmond, the leader of the Irish Parliamentary Party, had promised Irish help in Europe, and he, along with other leading nationalist figures, had played an active role in the recruiting campaign. There had been considerable sympathy at the outset for the plight of Belgium, a Catholic nation, at the mercy of Germany. However, as disillusionment with trench warfare set in, helped by the British government's refusal to allow the Southern Irish to have their own brigade and insignia, enthusiasm for the war effort declined rapidly. The growing fear of conscription, from which, for the time being, Ireland had been exempted, deepened Ireland's hostility to the war.

65   Alfred Deale and his brother Edwin Deale (the organist) were closely involved with the Methodist Church. Alfred was a choirmaster there, and also had his own business: he was described as a paper and twine merchant, a printer and stationer.

66   Herbert Park.

ing down the road, and prisoners taken, had not, he said, had any shave as close. Of course I did not tell them at home.[67]

Thursday, April 27th, after lunch

In the forenoon I was down at Morehampton Road shop. All there was normal but supplies somewhat limited. Afterwards down at Baggot St (Upper). Many shops were closed and supplies in many were running out. No meat. Got the last Oxtongue and 2 Mutton Kidneys at Butchers, all meat commandeered by military. Carried home, 2 stone Potatoes and meat, everybody out carrying home their own stores.[68]

Very serious fighting round Northumberland Road and down Mount Street (Lr), Clanwilliam Place, Boland Bakery reported blown down. Many casualties in to R.C.D. [Royal City of Dublin] Hospital. Rumoured that Richmond Hospital is in possession of S.Fs and Sir Thomas Myles (correct) & Dr McConnell (incorrect) [these two words in brackets were later amendments by the author] detained to look after their wounded.[69]

67 Other contemporary accounts tell similar stories of lucky escapes for Dublin citizens (e.g., diary of the Dublin shopkeeper, John Clarke, NLI, MS 10485; Mrs Arthur Mitchell's letter to her sister, NLI, MS 24553).
68 Dubliners were much put out by the interruption to their lives, and one of the main problems they felt was the serious shortage of food supplies, and the bread queues; bread was particularly scarce because of the insurgents' occupation of one of Dublin's main bakeries, Boland's. Difficulties in getting provisions was one of the main themes in the account of the Rising by Mrs Mitchell of Herbert Park: 'The shops were like a siege, all closed, and only a few women let in at a time and only small quantities of things being sold to each customer. I could only get a quarter stone of flour and half a stone of oatmeal, but I took all I could get, and two ribs of beef. Arthur and I staggered home laden. Other people in the Park were for food and some had been left bread-less' (Mrs Arthur Mitchell's letter to her sister, NLI, MS 24553). These entries are examples of the effects of the Rising on middle-class lives. One of the temporary social effects of the Rising was that middle-class *men* had to go out to get provisions. Another effect was that people from different classes talked together in the streets. See pp. 4, 44 & note 102 below.
69 Sir Thomas Myles (former President of the Royal College of Surgeons) and Dr

About 11.30 we saw small parties of troops resting on the road across the Park. Violet immediately obsessed with the idea that there would be fighting in the Park. I went down and talked to them. They said they were halted on their way into town. They said they would be attacking and only wished the S.Fs would come out into the Park into the open. After a little they began to march across the Park on to Morehampton Road and so on into town. The tension was relieved when we saw the long lines of perhaps 2000 men with carts, kitchens and cyclists, R. Engineers, and one or two guns off the fleet on lorries. Sylvia gave them fruit as they passed at the gate[70] but what we had in the house was very little, and we knew the shops were running short. The afternoon had been quiet, no firing in the neighbourhood and not much in the distance. F.H. Browning died last night, very sad for the poor little wife and Jeffrey.

A.A. McConnell (Ireland's first neural surgeon) were both surgeons at the Richmond Hospital and lived in the fashionable squares near the centre of Dublin – the former in Merrion and the latter in Fitzwilliam Square. Myles was a life-long nationalist, and had taken part in a gun-running episode for the Volunteers in 1914, but he did not approve of the Rising, which he considered rash. He cared for the wounded on both sides, though did perhaps display some partisanship towards the insurgents (J.B. Lyons, *An assembly of Irish surgeons* [Dublin, 1984], pp. 14-15).

70   Sylvia was the author's daughter, aged thirteen-and-a-half. The British troops arriving from England were generally well received and were given tea and showered with presents of chocolate, fruit, etc., on their journey from Kingstown. The details in the Fannin diary can be exactly corroborated by the account of another resident of Herbert Park, Mrs Mitchell, who was also distributing gifts at the same time. She wrote on the Thursday that at 11.30 she discovered about fifty soldiers resting in the Park, 'so after cogitating with myself came to the conclusion they were worthy objects, so sallied forth with the half box of cigarettes, and two dozen boxes of matches I had for the Soldiers Buffet, eighteen pieces of chocolate, and acid drops, and Sis and I distributed them. They were so grateful, and we could have done with twice the amount, other people were doing the same' (Mrs Arthur Mitchell's letter, MS 24553). John Dillon's account reiterates the initial lack of hostility to the troops: a Father Fahy had told him that when he first met officers and soldiers coming into Dublin they were afraid they would meet 'a solidly hostile population' and be sniped at from every house. Father Fahy had assured them that was a totally false impression, and that they would find the great majority of the people friendly - and officers had now come to realize that he was right (Dillon Papers, TCD, MS 9820).

Friday, April 28th

Plenty of talk and rumours but no definite news. About 1 o'clock
was at the R.C.D. Hospital. Went down in Red Cross Badged motor car to Grafton Street (41) to get Bandages and Lint for R.C.D.
Hospital. Streets clear to Upper Merrion Street. Then came into
area of military, troops were passing along the north side of Merrion
Square, two files one on each side of the road about four paces apart.
As they came opposite the end of Lower Merrion Street they ran
across the street as firing was going on in Westland Row, also in
Lower Mount Street and some houses in Merrion Square (but of
this I could not be sure). We had to pass Leinster Lawn, stop for
sentry at the foot of street and then into Clare Street. The files of
troops were turning into Lincoln Place and going down into
Westland Row or TCD We then ran along Nassau Street. Soldiers
stood at intervals of about 25/50 yards along the streets close to the
houses and railings on each side. There were also pickets at various
points. Then we turned up Grafton Street. It was absolutely deserted except for soldiers at intervals. The streets were full of straw
and rubbish from the looting of the street.[71] I was afraid of broken
glass from the tyres. We turned into Duke St, Anne Street and up
the back lane. I and the other man walked round to the front with
a soldier and in. Got out some Serum, Lint and Bandages, tumbled
them into the car and got away as quickly as possible. Came back
through Merrion St into Merrion Row, the nearest point to the

71 Most contemporary accounts of the Rising stress the extensive looting that oc-
    curred in the city during that week, when the poor from the Dublin slums came
    out to raid the shops. John Dillon wrote from North George's Street that 'a steady
    stream of women, girls and young children have passed up this street, laden with
    loot – clothes, boots' (Dillon Papers, TCD, MS 9820). Toys, fruit and sweets were
    also particular favourites. J.R. Clegg of Rathgar recounts in his 'Citizen's Diary'
    that 'In Sackville Place an excited mob, women and boys, has broken into the
    stores there of Lawrence's toy and sports bazaar. The front of this establishment is
    still intact, but the mob have entered by this side street, and golf sticks, musical
    instruments, toys in boxes, dolls in boxes, and other things, are thrown out to the
    crowd below, who seize them and make bundles of them. This mob is augmented

Military control. We found Uncle Richard[72] and Tho[ma]s[73], also Dr Tweedy[74] for whom I wanted the Serum. I did not go far from home in the afternoon. More troops continually arriving.[75]

Saturday, April 29th

Saturday morning went as far as Upper Leeson Street. Saw Kenny re money for Grafton Street Wages.[76] Most of them had come to him for wages out of money he had taken out from Grafton Street on Thursday. On this day, Friday, there had been firing in Lr Fitzwilliam Street when Alfie was in his house. He thought it was

by more of women and girls from the slums. One woman with an immense bundle of plunder in a shawl drops on the footpath in Sackville Street and declares to her God that she can't carry it farther without a rest. Boys parade with golf sticks, air guns, toy drums.' Elsewhere, in Camden Street, he describes the strange image of odd dress shoes being kicked about the pavements. Both sides did take some action to try to curb the looting. Clegg noted that the soldiers were shooting up Grafton Street for this purpose, though the main pillaging occurred in the North side of the city, and a Dubliner observed as he walked up Grafton Street how little damage there was there, apart from some attempted looting. Many were shocked by the looting, and one contemporary account which was generally sympathetic to the insurgents commented that '*hell won't be hot enough* for those looters'; but this was written by a shopkeeper (John Clarke's diary of the Rising, NLI, MS 10485; *Irish Times*, 2 May 1916). See also p. 41 and note 95 below.

72 Richard Booth was the author's uncle on his mother's side. Because of the death of Alfred and Edward's father while they were still in their teens, Booth had played an influential role in their lives. See above, introduction, p. 6, and note 32.

73 Possibly a nephew of Richard Booth's (or Sir Thomas Myles).

74 Ernest H. Tweedy was a well-known doctor at St Steven's Hospital, and he lived in Fitzwilliam Place.

75 The fighting strength for the British forces in Dublin at the start of the Rising was *c.* 2400 soldiers; by the end of the first day troops from the Curragh had increased the number to 4000; by the end of the Tuesday, men from Athlone, Templemore and Belfast made it 6600. By the Friday two Brigades from England (the North Midlands) had arrived at Kingstown to bring the total number of British troops in Dublin to 16,000.

76 It is worth noting that the author is concerned to ensure that his employees receive their wages, and that, despite the extraordinary circumstances, the running of the business continued to be of prime importance to him. The interruption of normal commercial life seems to have been one of his main reactions to the Rising: see below, p. 51, note 117 and also introduction, pp. 6-7.

almost next door and feared he was cut off at the front of the house. Either the soldiers were in [the] corner house of Upper Mount St and Fitzwilliam and were firing at the S.Fs on Steevens Church[77] or Baggot St Convent or houses in Lr Mount Street or vice versa. Ulimately got home from the rear. On Saturday morning Jameson Johnson[78] was stopped in Lr Baggot St at Dr Rowlette's[79] door by 15 armed Sinn Feiners on bicycles. 2 of them called to put his hands up, which he did. He was then searched, told that some S.Fs had been fired on by Red Cross. While being searched, he asked to be allowed to move closer to the wall so as to be shielded from the fire of a party of soldiers at Sir Thomas Myles' house facing up the street. Most of the men then cycled down Lr Fitzwilliam Street to the arch facing Sir Arthur Ball's house[80] and opened fire on the military down the street. When they had drawn the fire, they slipped on to the bicycles and went off. During the night we all were rather wakeful, there were some immense crashing explosions. And it is now reported that Clerys also is down,[81] also that the G.P.O. has

77   St Steevens (Stephen's) Church is also known as the Peppercanister Church.
78   George Jameson Johnston was Professor of Surgery at the Royal College of Surgeons and was also a surgeon and lecturer at the R.C.D. Hospital. Along with Alfred Fannin, he was one of the 763 citizens who in the aftermath of the Rising were to sign a petition which for 'the preservation of peace in Ireland' protested 'against any interference with the discretion of the Commander in Chief of the Forces in Ireland during the operation of Martial Law' (Asquith Papers, Bodleian, MS 42, ff. 90-137). See also above, introduction, p. 7.
79   Robert J. Rowlette was a doctor at Jervis Street Hospital, Lower Baggot Street.
80   Sir Arthur Ball was a surgeon at Sir Patrick Dun's Hospital, Lower Fitzwilliam Street.
81   Clery's was a major department store in Dublin (and was known as the Harrods, or sometimes the Selfridges, of Dublin); it was situated in Sackville Street, almost opposite the G.P.O., and would thus be a victim of the shelling that was aimed at the insurgents' headquarters. It was in flames on the Thursday night in the huge fires that raged in the Lower Abbey Street/Sackville Street area. A Red Cross driver told Douglas Hyde that the front wall of Clery's was standing without any back or roof or sides (Douglas Hyde's diary, TCD, MS 10343/7). Looting of its contents during the Rising was notorious, but, above all, it was the burning of Sackville Street that had the most impact on Dubliners. Henry Hanna concluded his narrative of the Rising with the comment that 'when it was all over, one could never forget half-burnt, ruined Sackville Street which looked as if it had stood a siege' (TCD, MS 10066/192). Strangely enough the great fires in the city and the

been taken. The day wore slowly away and towards evening the news came that the Sinn Feiners had made an unconditional surrender.[82] This is, of course, provisionally speaking. The revolt is too widespread to be stopped in a minute but it gave some hope for a peaceful Sunday.[83] It seemed that the leaders had surrendered but that different posts might hold out. We hoped that during the evening as the news filtered through the different posts things would quiet. About 8 P.M. we heard 3 explosions which sounded very close. Afterwards heard these were the blowing in of railings or houses at the Dispensary, Ballsbridge immediately opposite R.D.S. (Headquarters of Brigade). Snipers had got in there. Throughout the night there was firing, at first only occasional shots some of which seemed very near. The wind had changed and gone East so that we heard shooting from that quarter more distinctly but through the night the fighting seemed only from the quarter Ballsbridge to Ringsend and Sandymount. I did not hear very much but Violet and Emma said there was a good deal.

sight of Sackville Street are not mentioned in the Fannin diary, emphasizing, perhaps, that his impressions of the Rising were based on his experience of the South side of the city. He does not appear to have ventured northwards across the Liffey, reasons of safety and the difficulty in getting past military checkpoints being two obvious explanations for this. See above, pp. 27–8, 34–6. Several contemporary accounts tell of the fires making a 'blood red sky at night'. Mrs Arthur Mitchell of Herbert Park wrote: 'the city is in flames in many places like Sodom and Gomorrha; and it makes one feel quite *sick*', while the Dublin shopkeeper, John Clarke, described how, on the nights of Thursday, Friday and Saturday, 'the heavens were red with the glare of the fires . . . the flames were much higher than all roofs.' These must surely have been visible from Herbert Park (Monk Gibbon's account, Mrs Arthur Mitchell's letter, John Clarke's diary, NLI, MSS 5808, 24553, 10485).

82 By the end of the week insurgents from many of the outposts had joined the forces in the G.P.O., which had, naturally, become the main target of attack from the British troops; it was evacuated on the Friday, and Connolly and Pearse took up position in nearby Moore Street. When it became apparent that the odds were hopelessly against them, and to save further loss of life, the two leaders called for an unconditional surrender on the Saturday.

83 This comment reflects the strength of the family's religious commitment and, no doubt, the hope that their regular church attendance on the Sunday and normal Sunday life would not be interrupted.

Sunday morning, April 30th

Sniping shots still go on, some sounding very close. A Policeman passes asking the safest way to Ballsbridge, says a sniper is in St Bartholomew's Tower. (This rumour was out before.) One would say it was a hard place to clear out of but a desperate man might choose it. Alfie telephoned that there had been fighting in Sandymount Avenue. 2 houses had been blown up by the military to clear it of S.Fs. We were to keep under shelter of the return of the house. The patrol at Ballsbridge is more keen today and we are not allowed past the far end of the Park.

Uncle Richard went to London on Friday night for the Annual W.M.S. [Wesleyan Missionary Society] Meeting.[84] I gave him orders for Tetanus Antitoxin and was delighted to see Coade turning up this (Sunday) morning back from London with a gross of it. I have found it very hard to get it distributed owing to the Military patrols.[85] Thus when you get to any of the canal bridges into town you may be at once turned back, even if you do get through you may be held up inside by fighting or sniping.[86] Today (Sunday) all is quiet except at Ballsbridge and to a certain extent around Richmond Hill.[87]

---

84   This gives an interesting insight into the Booth family's Methodist connections, for Richard Booth was intent on keeping his commitment to the W.M.S. meeting in London, despite the Rising. (See above, introduction, p. 7.)

85   Alfred Fannin was determined to keep essential medical supplies going – he undoubtedly recognized the responsibility of the medical profession and their suppliers (like Fannins) in the Rising, and this diary does stress their role. Douglas Hyde commented in his account on the importance of the doctors: 'during the first days of fighting it was sufficient for a doctor to hold up his hand, and firing would cease when he went to attend the wounded' (Douglas Hyde's diary, TCD, MS 10343/7).

86   It had been a central part of the insurgents' plan to control the bridges over the canal; sniping accounted for many of the injuries.

87   Richmond Hill was in the South part of the city, near the Portobello Barracks.

Dublin after the 1916 Rising (*courtesy of* the National Library of Ireland).
Above: North Earl Street. *Below*: Sackville Street and Eden Quay.

Sunday afternoon, April 30th 1916

Alfie has spoken today to the Lord Mayor[88] who confirms what has been said about the centres of the rebellion being crushed.

On Saturday morning the King's Royal Rifles made an attack on the G.P.O. The Guns were brought up and the building shelled. A message was brought to the O/C that the Post Office wished to surrender on terms. The O/C wrote something like this. "A message has been brought by this woman that you desire to surrender. If this is the case, you alone will leave the building accompanying this woman under a flag of truce and proceed to Moore Street where you will be met: the only terms will be those of unconditional surrender." At the time arranged for surrender the rebels were ordered to march out in single file: this reached from Nelson's Pillar to the Rotunda: then to halt: ground arms: take off bandoliers: empty their pockets: and march off. The military collected the arms and ammunition.[89] Pearse, the Provisional President,[90] and Connolly, the officer commanding in Dublin,[91] were in charge. As soon as the street was clear, people were out of the houses in the street to collect trophies from the pockets of the volunteers.[92]

88   The Lord Mayor was James M. Gallagher.
89   The woman mentioned here is Nurse Elizabeth O'Farrell (one of three women who had remained with Connolly and Pearse throughout the Rising); she acted as intermediary between the leaders and the British forces, until Connolly and Pearse agreed to unconditional surrender.
90   Padraic Pearse, with his belief in the 'blood sacrifice', had been the main inspiration behind the Rising. He had also been the IRB Director of Military Operations, and, as head of the Provisional Government of the Irish Republic, delivered the Proclamation of Independence from the steps of the G.P.O. on Easter Monday.
91   James Connolly was a committed socialist who had played a leading role in the Irish Transport and General Workers Union and in the Dublin lock-out of 1913. He, as organizer of the Irish Citizen Army, and military commander of the insurgents in Dublin, had been, along with Pearse, the main architect of the Rising. See also note 7 above.
92   Elsie Mahaffy, the daughter of TCD's Provost, told in her account of the Rising how the body of The O'Rahilly (the co-founder and Director of Arms of the Irish Volunteers) had been found wrapped in the flag of the Irish Republic: 'Romantic

About the same time the Four Courts were taken by the Military, only portions of the buildings remain. [Author's later insertion: Incorrect – the damage is trifling.] On Friday and Saturday nights a good deal of civilian clothing was handed in to Jacobs. The rebels have learned the danger of a uniform. A good deal of changing was done and on Sunday afternoon a surrender was arranged, but it was found that nearly all the rebels had escaped.[93] As was natural, a great deal of looting was done here. Moffitt[94] saw men emptying sacks of flour into the aprons of women as he passed on Sunday afternoon.[95]

Earlier on Sunday the College of Surgeons surrendered. They had sent over to Vincent's Hospital to see if they would accept Sinn Fein wounded. They replied they had already Military wounded in and could not have the others (except as prisoners, I infer). Then could they send over doctors? Two of the younger doctors were ready to go but Tobin[96] told them that the place might at any moment be rushed or blown up by the Military and if so they would almost certainly be sacrificed, so they did not go. [These last two sentences were amended with the author's marginal comment: Doubtful if this was true.] A little later the Countess Markievicz

ladies thought this touching until it became known that under the flag, he was stark naked. His watch, his pearl pin, his clothes were all rifled off his dead body', (TCD, MS 2074). See note 10 above.

93 According to the *Irish Times'* report of the surrender at Jacob's Factory, a member of the Carmelite Order persuaded the insurgents to give themselves up: he was hauled up to one of the windows, and shortly afterwards the Volunteers walked out, many of them in civilian dress, which had been smuggled into them (*Sinn Fein Rebellion Handbook*, p. 26).

94 Moffitt was a long-serving member of Fannin's firm.

95 The *Irish Times* noted on 2 May that after the surrender and evacuation of the Volunteers at Jacob's Factory, 'the crowd then indulged in looting on an extensive scale, many bags of flour and boxes of biscuits being carried off'. Douglas Hyde, however, stressed that the extraordinary thing about Jacob's was that the Volunteers left the machinery and everything else in complete order so that it would be possible for work to restart there the following morning; they had also tried to stop the looting (Douglas Hyde's diary, 1 May, TCD, MS 10343/7).

96 Richard Tobin was a surgeon at St Vincent's Hospital.

surrendered and she and about 100 S.Fs were marched down Grafton Street as prisoners.

This same Sunday afternoon the rebels in Boland's Bread Bakery sent word over to Sir P. Dun's Hospital to know if it was all right for them to give in. As their leader (Dolores or some such name) [Author's marginal note added later: De Valera][97] explained, "The military will not respect the white Flag"!! They then came out and were marched down to Ballsbridge to the number of about 80.

Monday, May 1st

The Position on Monday May 1st then is that practically all the main posts of the rebels on the South Side of the city, except the Gas Works, have surrendered. Fighting therefore is still proceeding at this point and in addition sniping on the roofs is going on at Merrion Square, Baggot St, Northumberland Road, Mount Street, Harcourt Road, anywhere in fact where there are tall houses of even height so that it is easy for soldiers and S.Fs to pass from roof to roof. This is going on in many places, terrifying for the inhabitants and making the ordinary business of the city impossible. How soon this can be put down it is impossible to foresee. There were rumours of all sorts during the week: of an attempted landing of the Germans at Lowestoft and of the sinking of their transports and the escape of its escort, our loss [of] about 14 ships, of the German Fleet at last coming out to give battle, of an engagement in which both sides lose heavily but in which we have the greater

---

97   De Valera's forces had been the last to surrender. He was one of the few leaders to escape execution, and he was subsequently President of the transformed Sinn Fein. The fact Fannin was unable to write de Valera's name correctly is further confirmation of how little was known about the Rising's leaders, and is also an indication that, at this stage, de Valera was one of the less prominent of the organizers and commandants. See also note 7 above.

success. Today's rumour (Monday May 1st) is that cannonading has been heard at sea and that the Germans are trying to land at Kingstown.

Perhaps you will realise that while those at a distance (i.e. in England) might think that the tension is easier today, Monday, the fact is that it is really only some degrees less so long as the firing continues round us and so many rumours abound.[98] During the end of the last week we have heard of the fall of Kut[99] and yet we cared little so long as the rebels here give in. The nearer bulked the bigger so far as we in Dublin were concerned.

At ordinary times we hate the chiming of St Bartholomew's every quarter hour and its out-of-tune hymn tunes at intervals. Throughout this week we have felt it the one thing permanent and regular apart of course from the forces of Nature and the work of God.[100] The weather throughout has been beautiful. Mild early summer with brilliant sunshine all the week after a long cold spring.[101]

98 This rumour, that the Germans had landed in Ireland, was a particular favourite and can be found in several other contemporary accounts, e.g. Thomas Johnsons's (see bibliography). This rumour was believed for a while by the insurgents in Jacob's Factory, where thirty minutes of cheering broke out until the truth was known, and also in the G.P.O., where British shelling was taken for the sound of German guns. See above, pp. 23–5 and notes 9, 34, 43.

99 Fannin would have read of the fall of Kut-al-Amara in the *Irish Times* of 2 May. As part of the Mesopotamia campaign in the war, General Townshend had advanced towards Baghdad and was besieged by the Turks at Kut with 10,000 men for many weeks. This was a major setback for Britain.

100 This particular passage is especially revealing and captures the impact of the Rising on a family like the Fannins. This desire to cling to some kind of normality was partially echoed in the *Irish Times*, and in TCD's attempt at 'business as usual'. John Dillon's diary has a similar conclusion: he got up at 5.00 A.M. on the Sunday morning: it was a lovely spring morning: 'Everything was quiet and peaceful – as if nothing had happened out of the normal.' Alfred Fannin had no real insight into the importance of the Rising for the course of Ireland's history – indeed, many would have been as yet unable to realize its significance, for it was really the aftermath that was of greater import (Dillon Papers, TCD, MS 9820). See introduction, p. 10 and notes 47 and 110.

101 The generally good weather during the Rising must have helped the insurgents, though (contrary to Alfred Fannin's statement) the weather was not entirely fine

We have all been well in spite of nerves abounding and I am sure you would smile to see the long lines of people carrying home loaves of bread across the Park from Johnston Mooney's (myself amongst them) or to see your humble servant with an armful of cauliflower returning from Upper Leeson Street. Butcher's meat is unobtainable for several days but we have some hope of a joint today or tomorrow. Of course the housekeepers here make a fair show in the flesh on very little, but if things go on as they are our ordinary scale of living must be greatly curtailed. Prices, however, have not risen much, showing that people expect normal conditions soon.[102]

all week. Douglas Hyde, for instance, commented that many Volunteers were in hospital with pneumonia which they had got as a result of fighting in heavy rain in St Stephen's Green on the Tuesday, but that was the only rain that fell in the week (Douglas Hyde's diary, TCD, MS 10343/7).

102 Other contemporary accounts contain very similar observations: Thomas Johnson wrote that: 'it is a strange sight to see hundreds of men, well-dressed, middle-class citizens, lugging home bags of flour, bundles of vegetables, rhubarb, cabbage, etc. Most of the shops are sold out of goods. No bread is available today.' A Dublin shopkeeper, John Clarke, told how all the shops were closed, though a few small ones in the side streets would open briefly if they had any stock; for the first time in their life they had had to use condensed milk. For the *Irish Times* 'many amusing scenes were witnessed, and it was a novel sight to see well-known clergymen, professional and commercial men, passing along struggling with bundles of cauliflowers, cabbage, meat, biscuits, bread, and a thousand and one other articles, which, in ordinary times would be sent home in receptacles more imposing than a wrapping of old newspapers.' Thomas King Moylan of Rathgar described the extraordinary spectacle of 'all the toffs and lady toffs' carrying home their cottage loaf, 'without even a scrap of newspaper to hide its nakedness'. The poor of Dublin, however, did not fare so well, and they had severe problems getting hold of any food. The TCD student Eileen Corrigan recounted how she helped distribute free bread tickets to the poor in Rathmines, many of whom then queued all day to receive their loaves from the Town Hall. Fannin may not have been totally accurate with his comment that prices 'have not risen much': The *Irish Times* reported severe rises for butter, potatoes, meat – though, support for Fannin's view can be found in the paper's comment that the better-class shops did not increase the mutton price that much, and that once it was known that vegetable supplies were obtainable from outside the centre, prices were quickly restored to nearly the former level. Moreover, Fannin had probably not felt the rise in prices during the week to be very significant when compared to the overall rise in agricultural prices in Ireland brought about by the onset of World War (Thomas Johnson's diary published in J.A. Gaughan, *Thomas Johnson*, p. 53; John Clarke's diary, NLI, MS 10485; *Irish Times*,

Saturday, May 6th

These notes end with Monday May 1st. I have delayed to send them till today, Saturday May 6th, as full postal communication is only now being gradually resumed. I have sent you the daily papers giving much fuller and more correct accounts of the rebellion.[103] Reading the notes now they seem unduly introspective, [it] is only from the point of view of one who stayed at 32 H.Pk [Herbert Park] all the time.[104] They are only for your own reading and you will make allowances for the point of view taken, also correct the history by the daily paper.

Your letters written to Violet & myself, April 26th, and Norah's to Auntie only to hand. Shall pay accounts and send on receipts. City

    2 May 1916; T.K. Moylan, 'A Dubliner's Diary, 1914–1918', 1 May 1916, NLI, MS 9620 (all reasonable effort has been made to trace the owner of this diary); Eileen Corrigan's account, *Belfast Evening Telegraph*, 5 May 1916).

103 Given the confusion and the many rumours circulating in Dublin, the accuracy of the press reports can be questioned, see J. Lee, *Ireland, 1912–1985*, p. 30; but the *Irish Times*, the paper Alfred Fannin would have almost certainly sent to his brother, did have a reputation for good reporting (O.D. Edwards, 'The *Irish Times* on the Easter Rising', in O.D. Edwards & F. Pyle, *1916: The Easter Rising* [London, 1968], pp. 241–3).

104 Postal services would have had to be re-established after the destruction of the G.P.O. On 2 May J.R.Clegg concluded his 'Citizen's Diary' in the *Irish Times* with a poignant comment about the impact of the week on Dubliners, and above all about their sense of isolation; the war; 'the severance for such a length of time of all communication with places outside the city; the complete lack of communications inside; the absence of the daily papers; the disappearance of the police; the cessation of the tramcar and other wheeled traffic; the problem of getting house supplies; the total shortage of business; the vague and often alarming reports of casualties; the paucity of authentic information; the unfamiliar and menacing detonations, night and day . . . gave an unprecedentedly strange colour to the daily life of Dublin.' Alfred Fannin's diary has captured the feelings underlying these words.

is quiet now. Military Passes[105] no longer needed but all must be into their houses at 7.30.[106]

With Love from all to Both,

Yours affectionately,

Alfie
(May 6, 1916)

Please keep this letter for me. I intended to copy it but am too lazy.

> 41 Grafton St ⎫
> & 3 Rutland Square ⎬   quite safe[107]

105   The roads in the area of the Fannins' house, and between Herbert Park and the centre, had become proscribed areas, and no one could get in or out without considerable difficulty. Passes were only given to those who were considered to be 'essential' – Fannin and his brother-in-law would have had little trouble obtaining these because of their medical role.

106   Under martial law, Dubliners had to remain indoors from 7.30 p.m. to 5.00 A.M.

107   No. 3, Rutland Square, a fashionable place for professionals to live (now known as Parnell Square), was Edward Fannin's house.

Dear Ed

I hope you got my long letter all right about the rebellion. Every thing feels strangely quiet ever since. There are enormous numbers of soldiers about and we are to have a division quartered now in the Phoenix Park. The papers will have given you a fair idea of what took place but the feelings of those who went through it must be imagined. The experiences of the G.Rs were very tragic. I explained what happened to the lot that went by Northumberland Road. The other lot, Harris's, were fired on between Shelbourne Road and the front gate of Beggars Bush, one or two were killed and the remainder got to the gate or over the wall.[108] To defend Beggars Bush there were 7 soldiers, mostly crocks. 100 or so of G.Rs with only 13 rifles all told amongst the lot. They tried to make the live rifles look as many as they could. But if the Sinn Feiners had rushed them they could easily have wiped them out. Geo[rge] Beckett & Connell of Belfast Bank were among them. They had to lie all night under the walls of the Barracks in the hope that if the S.Fs came they might knock in their heads at close quarters before they could shoot. Late on Tuesday afternoon an armoured motor car came into the barracks with rifles and on Wednesday a party of the Sherwood Foresters fought their way in to the barracks, but up till the Wednesday of next week they could not leave the barracks and were being sniped

108 Major G.A. Harris of the TCD O.T.C. was Commanding Officer of the G.Rs. See above, note 17 for a fuller account of this whole incident. When the group under Harris reached Shelbourne Road, they were warned they would find it difficult to get into the barracks. Some tried to crawl round to the entrance, but shots were fired, so most decided to scramble over the wall. (See the account of a participant, Henry Hanna, TCD, MS 10066/192.)

all the time.[109] The G.Rs in Beggars Bush and the O.T.C. in College were the two exciting times of the rebellion.[110] Although Kearney in Stephen's Green showed as much pluck as any one. The S.Fs seized the Green and ordered him to leave on pain of shooting. He said, "I have five sons in the army and I'm not going to do any thing that would make them ashamed of me. I've been 30 years in Stephen's Green and I am going to stay" and he did.[111]

We are still under martial law.[112] There have been a good many

109   Henry Hanna has given a detailed first-hand account of the defence of the barracks, in which he was involved. The barracks was not a regular military establishment, and there were only two young officers of the Regulars and their sole defence consisted of 16 service rifles, as there was no ammunition to fit the rifles that most of the men were using, which were of an older or foreign style. Few knew how to use the service rifles. Thus, poorly armed, they yet managed to hold off the insurgents until help came from the Sherwood Foresters. Hanna commented that food was short for a time, and 'when they came out the men all looked older and thinner, as the strain had been great' (TCD, MS 10066/192).
110   Trinity College was a unit of the O.T.C., and had plenty of ammunition. A number of members of the College decided that it had to be defended; the O.T.C. Lieutenant, G. Waterhouse, Professor of German, took charge and ordered the gates to be shut. With about fifty men Trinity was defended for over twenty-four hours until British troops from the Curragh arrived. The expected attack from the insurgents never materialized. Professor A.A. Luce, who was at that time home on leave from France after measles, recalled some fifty years later his involvement in the defence of Trinity. The College, trying to adopt a 'business as usual' approach, actually asked Luce to conduct a *viva voce* in logic, but he declined (TCD, MS 4874). Further evidence that Trinity tried to continue a normal life is provided in the account by the third-year student, Eileen Corrigan, who sat her exams in college on the Tuesday and Wednesday of the Rising (*Belfast Evening Telegraph*, 5 May 1916).
111   Kearney is mentioned earlier in the diary, see above, p. 28 and note 57. The sentiments expressed here were fairly typical of many Dubliners who had relatives fighting in the Great War and who saw the Rising as a betrayal of their efforts.
112   The imposition and continuance for a considerable time of martial law was one of the main factors which alienated the Irish population, especially Dubliners from the British authorities. Civil government had been destroyed by the Rising, and though there was an attempt to restore it with the appointment of H.E. Duke as Chief Secretary, General Maxwell was really the man in control, and he was not removed until November. However, some of the better-off citizens of Dublin, Cork, etc. (Fannin included), motivated by a desire for peace and stability, petitioned the government that there should be no interference in Maxwell's operation of martial law (Asquith Papers, Bodleian, MS 42, ff. 90–137). See above, introduction p. 7 and note 78.

executions[113] and we all must be in at 8.30 at night but the city by day is resuming its normal appearance. I was in Rutland Square the other day. You have one bullet hole in your drawing room window. The bullet made a round hole in the glass, splintered at edges, went through blind, hit the wall about shoulder high at edge of wood door frame near fireplace leaving a mark in plaster about 1 in. diameter and 1 in. deep, rebounded across the room and was found in the fold of the curtain at foot of window through which it had first come. I shall post you the bullet.[114]

Ewie has been getting steadily better, the gland in his neck is nearly smooth now, and today Violet, Sylvia and he have gone down to Salthill Co. Galway to spend a week with the George Parsons.[115] This had been the plan all through but the rebellion interfered. They may stay a week after the Parsons come up if they can find suitable quarters. At the moment Auntie[116] and I are all alone in the house. The gas has been off [in] the city since the Rebellion and so until today they had no gas in Fitzwilliam St and Mrs Parsons and Emma stayed here. Of course they had come to help to nurse

---

113 After the Rising, ninety death sentences were passed, but for seventy-five of these (including Countess Markievicz and de Valera) the sentences were commuted to penal servitude. However, fifteen were still carried out, and it is these executions which played the major role in turning Irish public opinion against England and towards the goal of an independent Irish Republic that the leaders had sought. Some could see this as the fulfilment of Pearse's 'blood sacrifice'. At the time of this letter (10 May) thirteen had been shot, including Pearse; it was the shooting two days later of Connolly – who had to sit because he was too wounded in the ankle to stand – that particularly horrified Dubliners.

114 The *Irish Times* commented on 2 May that the Rutland Square area was one of the most dangerous places for sniping, and that there had been a number of fatalities in the area. The diary of the shopkeeper, John Clarke, has a similar story about a bullet: while he was in a tailor's he witnessed an extraordinary sight – 'a shot came through their window, crossed the room, pierced the right wall *behind* a figure of B.V. [the Blessed Virgin] under a glass shade, neither were injured, most wonderful . . . ' (NLI, MS 10485).

115 George Parsons was Violet Fannin's brother.

116 'Auntie' was Alethea Fannin, who kept house for Edward Fannin at Rutland Square.

April 25th. 1916

Dear Ed

It is 10.30 A.M. Easter Tuesday morning and I have not gone in to business. I am detained at home with nothing to do and sit down to write some account of what happened yesterday in Dublin.

We had planned for golf at Greystones and at 10 yesterday morning. Emma & Helen Crawford Alfie & I in Alfie's motor. We were to meet Edwin & Edith at Greystones. Their car broke down and they did not get down till lunch time. I played a single with Helen. and in the afternoon. Emma & Alf played a single again & Helen & I played Edith & Ed. At lunch time one of the men at the clubhouse tried to telephone to town but was told that the wire into town was cut that the Sinn Feiners were out and had occupied Westland Row Station. Although there had been some rumours during the week of trouble with the S.Fs Noone had thought there was anything in it. Balfour and Emma played 9 holes after lunch and started for town about 4 o'clock, reaching town about 5. P.M they came to Herbert Park and heard that Violet & her mother had heard shots during

---

First page of manuscript of Alfred Fannin's 'Diary'.

Eustace. We lost you may say a clear fortnight's business over the troubles. I have paid all the staff in full which will mean £70 to £80 out of pocket in addition to the loss of trade.[117] Auntie continues quite well.

With Love to Both,

Your affectionate brother,

Alf

---

117 One of the most revealing aspects of this particular diary is the concern the author felt over the interruption to business, and it is perhaps significant that the diary begins and closes on this note. His desire that his staff should be fairly treated is again demonstrated.

SELECT BIBLIOGRAPHY

Published Accounts and Intepretations of the 1916 Rising

Caulfield, M., *The Easter Rebellion* (London, 1965)

Coffey, T., *Agony at Easter. The 1916 Irish Uprising* (London, 1970)

Cooney, D.A.L., 'Momentous days: occasional diaries of Francis Taylor', *Dublin Historical Record*, xlvii, pp. 77–86, 1994

Dhonnchadha, M. Ní & T. Dorgan (eds), *Revising the Rising* (Derry, 1991)

Duff, C. St Lawrence, *Six days to shake an empire: events and factors behind the Irish rebellion of 1916 – an account of that rebellion and its suppression and of the final struggle for self-govenment* (London, 1966)

Hally, P.J., 'The Easter 1916 Rising in Dublin; the military aspects', *The Irish Sword*, vii, pp. 313 ff. and viii, pp. 48 ff., 1966–67

Irish Times, 25 April – 3 May 1916; 'A Citizen's Diary' (J.R. Clegg of Rathgar, Dublin), 2 May 1916; 7 April 1966

Johnson, Thomas, diary of the Rising, published in Gaughan, A.J., *Thomas Johnson*, pp. 46-57 (Dublin, 1980)

Kain, R., 'A diary of Easter Week: one Dubliner's experience', *Irish University Review*, x, 1980

Lynch, D., *The I.R.B. and the 1916 Insurrection* (ed. F. O'Donoghue, Cork, 1957)

McHugh, R. (ed.), *Dublin, 1916* (London, 1966) (collection of previously published contemporary accounts)

McKenzie, F.A., *The Irish Rebellion* (London, 1916)

McLoughlin, S., 'Memories of the Easter Rising, 1916', *Camillian Post*, xiii, 1948

Martin, F.X., '1916 – myth, fact and mystery', *Studia Hibernica*, vii, 1967

— 'The 1916 Rising – *Coup d'etat* or a "bloody protest"?', *Studia Hibernica*, viii, 1968

— (ed), 'Eoin McNeill on the 1916 Rising', *Irish Historical Studies*, Select Documents, Mar. 1961

Ó Briain, L., 'Saint Stephen's Green area', *Capuchin Annual*, pp. 219 ff., 1966

Ó Broin, L., *Dublin Castle and the 1916 Rising* (Dublin, 1966)

O'Casey, Sean, *The Plough and the Stars* (1926), *Collected Plays*, 1 (London, 1949)

Ó Dubhghaill, M., *Insurrection fires at Eastertide: a golden jubilee anthology of the Easter Rising* (Cork, 1966)

O'Higgins, B. (ed.), *The soldier's story of Easter Week* (Dublin, 1966)

O'Leary, J.J., day-by-day account in *Dublin Saturday Post*, 29 Apr., 6, 13 May 1916

O'Neill, F., Col., 'The battle of Dublin, 1916', *An Cosantóir*, xxvi, pp. 211 ff., 1966

Royal Commission on the Rebellion in Ireland, minutes of evidence and appendix of documents (London, 1916)

Ryan, D., *The Rising: The complete story of Easter Week* (Dublin, 1949)

Stephens, James, *The Insurrection in Dublin* (a first-hand account), first published in 1916; re-published: Adams, Michael (ed.) (Dublin, 1965), and Murphy, J.A. (ed. & introduction) (Gerrards Cross, 1978)

Thompson, W.I., *The imagination of an insurrection: Dublin, Easter 1916* (Oxford, 1967)
Townshend, C., 'The suppression of the Easter Rising', *Bullán*, i, 1994
Weekly Irish Times, Sinn Fein Rebellion Handbook (Dublin, 1917)
Wells, W. & Marlowe, N., *A history of the Irish rebellion of 1916* (London & Dublin, 1916)
West, T., *Horace Plunkett, co-operation and politics* (Gerrard's Cross, 1986), Plunkett's diary, pp. 145–56

Further collections of Articles

Edwards, O. D. & Pyle, F. (eds.) *1916: The Easter Rising* (London, 1968), especially:
  Edwards, O.D., 'American aspects of the Rising'
  — 'Press reaction to the Rising in general'
  — 'The *Irish Times* on the Easter Rising'
  Edwards, R.D., 'The achievement of 1916'
  Lyons, F.S.L., 'Decline and fall of the Nationalist Party'
  McCartney, D., 'Gaelic ideological origins of 1916'
  McHugh, R., 'The Catholic Church and the Rising'
  Nevin, D., 'The Irish Citizen Army'
Martin, F.X. (ed.), *Leaders and men of the Easter Rising* (London, 1967) especially:
  Falls, C., 'Maxwell, 1916, and Britain at war'
  Farrell, B., 'Markievicz and the women of the Revolution'
  MacDonagh, D., 'Plunkett and MacDonagh'
  McHugh, R., 'Casement and German help'
  Martin, F.X., '1916 - Revolution or Evolution?'
  Nowlan, K.B., 'Tom Clarke, MacDermott, and the I.R.B.'
  Ó Broin, L., 'Birrell, Nathan, and the men of Dublin Castle'
  O'Donoghue, F., 'Ceannt, Devoy, O'Rahilly, and the military plan'
  Ó Luing, S., 'Arthur Griffith and Sinn Fein'
  Thornley, D., 'Patrick Pearse - the evolution of a Republican'
  Whyte, J.H., '1916 - Revolution and Religion'
  Williams, T.D., 'Eoin MacNeill and the Irish Volunteers'
Nowlan, K.B. (ed.), *The making of 1916* (Dublin, 1969) especially:
  Boyle, J.W., 'Connolly, the Citizen Army and the Rising'
  Hayes-McCoy, G.A., 'A military history of the 1916 Rising'
  Wall, M., 'The background to the Rising, from 1914 until the issue of the countermanding order on Easter Saturday, 1916'
  — 'The plans and the countermand: the country and Dublin'
Williams, D. (ed.), *The Irish struggle, 1916–26* (London, 1966) especially:
  Lynch, P., 'The social revolution that never was'
  Martin, F.X., 'The origins of the Irish Rising of 1916'
  Ryan, D., 'Sinn Fein policy and practice (1916–26)'

On Some of the Main People Involved

Augustine Birrell:
Ó Broin, L. , *The Chief Secretary, Augustine Birrell* (London,1969)

Roger Casement:
Inglis, B., *Roger Casement* (New York, 1973)

Michael Collins:
Coogan, T.P., *Michael Collins* (London, 1990)

James Connolly:
Edwards, Ruth D., *James Connolly* (Dublin, 1981)
Greaves, C.D., *The life and times of James Connolly* (London, 1961)
Morgan, A., *James Connolly, a political biography* (Manchester, 1988)

Eamon de Valera:
Coogan, T.P., *De Valera - Long Fellow, Long Shadow* (London, 1993)
Dwyer,T.R., *Eamon de Valera* (Dublin, 1980)
Edwards, O.D., *Eamon de Valera* (Cardiff, 1987)
Longford, Lord & O'Neill, T.P., *Eamon de Valera* (Dublin, 1970)

John Dillon:
Lyons, F.S.L., *John Dillon, a biography* (London, 1968)

Arthur Griffith:
Davis, R., *Arthur Griffith* (Dundalk, 1976)
Younger, C., *Arthur Griffith* (Dublin, 1981)

Thomas MacDonagh
Parks, E.W. & A.W., *Thomas MacDonagh - the man, the patriot, the writer* (Athens, Georgia, 1967)

Eoin MacNeill:
Martin, F.X. & Byrne, F.J. (eds), *The scholar revolutionary, Eoin MacNeill* (Shannon, 1973)

Countess Markievicz:
Haverty, A., *Constance Markievicz; an independent life* (London, 1988)
Marreco, A., *The Rebel Countess: The life and times of Countess Markievicz* (London, 1967)
Norman D., *Terrible beauty: a life of Constance Markievicz* (1987)
Van Voris, J., *Constance de Markievicz* (Massachusetts, 1967)

The O'Rahilly
Bourke, M., *The O'Rahilly* (Tralee, 1967)
O'Rahilly, A., *Winding the Clock, O'Rahilly and the 1916 Rising* (Dublin, 1991)

Patrick Pearse:
Edwards, Ruth D., *Patrick Pearse: The triumph of failure* (London, 1977)
Ryan, D., *The man called Pearse* (Dublin, 1919)

Other Relevant Works

Boyce, D.G. (ed.), *The Revolution in Ireland, 1879–1923* (London, 1988)

Brady, C. (ed.), *Interpreting Irish History, the debate on historical revisionism* (Dublin, 1994)

Fitzpatrick, D., *Politics and Irish life, 1913–21* (Dublin, 1977)

Fox, R.M., *History of the Irish Citizen Army* (Dublin, 1943)

Holt, E., *Protest in arms. The Irish Troubles 1916–23* (London, 1960)

Lee, J.J., *Ireland 1912–1985. Politics and Society* (Cambridge, 1989), especially pp. 24-38

Martin, F.X. (ed.), *The Irish Volunteers, 1913–1915* (Dublin, 1963)

Ó Broin, L., *Revolutionary underground: the story of the Irish Republican Brotherhood, 1858–1924* (Dublin, 1976)

O'Donoghue, F., 'The failure of the German arms landing at Easter 1916', *Journal of the Cork Historical and Archaeological Society*, 1966

Phillips, W.A., *The revolution in Ireland, 1906–23* (London, 1923)

Ryan, D., *The 1916 poets* (Dublin, 1963)

Ryan, D. (ed.), *Labour and Easter Week* (Dublin, 1949)

Shaw, F., 'The canon of Irish history: a challenge', *Studies*, lvi, 1972

Townshend, C., *Political violence in Ireland: government and resistance since 1848* (Oxford, 1983)

Ward, A.J., *The Easter Rising: revolution and Irish nationalism* (Arlington Heights, Illinois, 1980)

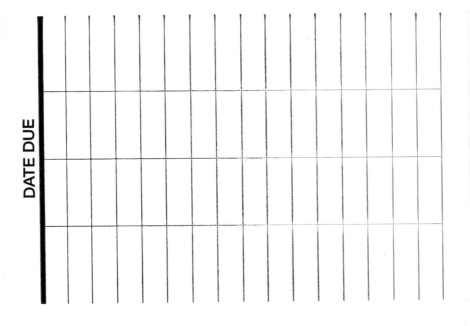